Adventures in Art

Laura H. Chapman

Davis Publications, Inc.

Worcester, Massachusetts

Printed in the United States of America
ISBN: 0-382-34209-7

2 3 4 5 6 7 8 9 10 WOR 01 00 99 98

Front cover: *Student artwork by James Brinkley, Bryant Elementary School, Mableton, Georgia. From the Crayola® Dream-Makers® Collection, courtesy of Binney & Smith Inc.*

Title page: *Joseph Stella,* Battle of Lights, Coney Island, *1913. Oil on canvas, 75 3/4 x 34" (192 x 89 cm). Yale University Art Gallery (Gift of Collection Société Anonyme).*

Editorial Advisory Board:

Dr. Cynthia Colbert
Professor of Art
and Chair of Art Education
University of South Carolina
Columbia, South Carolina

Bill MacDonald
Art Education Consultant
Vancouver, British Columbia
Canada

Dr. Connie Newton
Assistant Professor of Art
School of Visual Art
University of North Texas
Denton, Texas

Sandra Noble
Curriculum Specialist for the Fine Arts
Cleveland Public Schools
Cleveland, Ohio

Reading Consultant:

Dr. JoAnn Canales
College of Art Education
University of North Texas
Denton, Texas

Reviewers:

Cliff Cousins
Art Specialist
Davenport Community School District
Davenport, Iowa

Dr. Lila G. Crespin
College of Fine Art
California State University at
Long Beach

Lee Gage
Art Supervisor
Westchester Area School District
Westchester, Pennsylvania

William Gay, Jr.
Visual Art Coordinator
Richland County School District One
Columbia, South Carolina

Dr. Adrienne W. Hoard
Associate Professor
University of Missouri-Columbia

Mary Jordan
Visual Arts Curriculum Specialist
Tempe, Arizona

Kathleen Lockhart
Curriculum & Instructional Specialist
Baltimore, Maryland

David McIntyre
Consultant for Visual Arts
El Paso Independent School District
El Paso, Texas

R. Barry Shauck
Supervisor of Art
Howard County Public School
Ellicott City, Maryland

Linda Sleight
Visual Arts Curriculum Specialist
Tempe, Arizona

Carl Yochum
Director of Fine Arts
Ferguson-Florissant School District
Florissant, Missouri

Joyce Young
Assistant Principal
Bond Hill School
Cincinnati, Ohio

Acknowledgements:
The author and publisher would like to thank the following individuals and groups for their special assistance in providing images, resources and other help: Tom Feelings, Mickey Ford, Claire Mowbray Golding, Colleen Kelley, Samella Lewis, Maya Nigrosh, Sandra Palmer, Dawn Reddy, Tara Reddy, Patricia A. Renick, Chloë Sayer, Martha Siegel, Martin Speed, Bernice Steinbaum, Anne Straus, and art teachers in the Department of Defense Dependent Schools.

Managing Editor:
Wyatt Wade

Editor:
Laura J. Marshall

Design:
Douglass Scott, WGBH Design

Production:
Nancy Dutting

Photo Acquisitions:
Allan Harper

Illustrator:
Susan Christy-Pallo

Photography:
Schlowsky Photography

Contents

Page

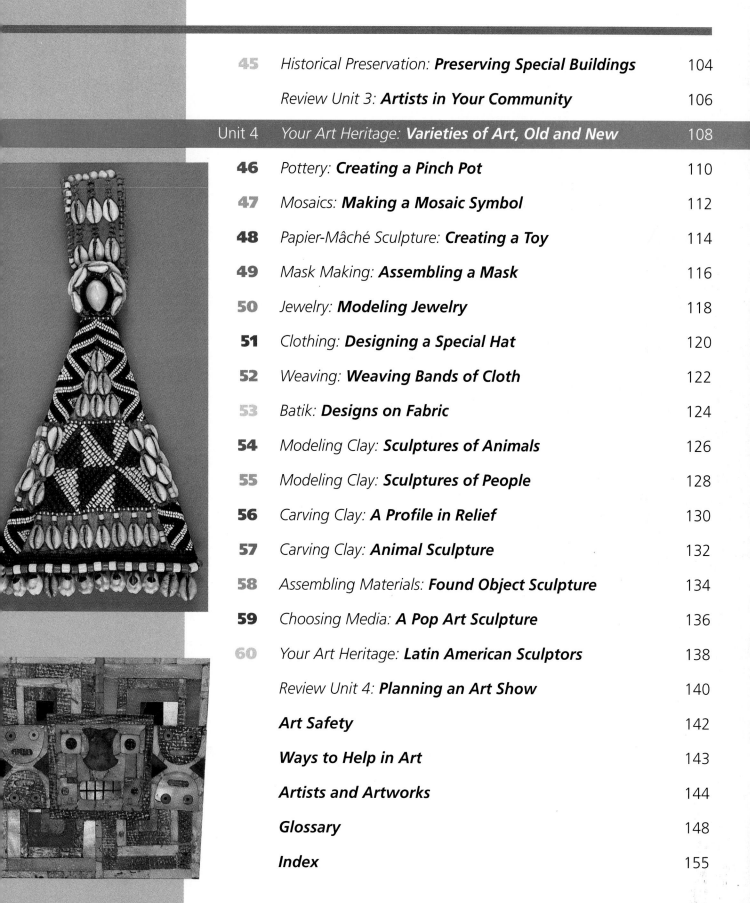

Janet Fish, *Orange Bowls and Yellow Pitcher,* 1979. Oil on canvas, 60 x 70" (152 x 178 cm). Robert Miller Gallery, New York.

You can communicate with people by writing words. Long before people invented writing, they communicated by making sounds and using hand signals. They also communicated by making pictures. They sent and received "wordless" messages.

Today, most people think about **art** as a way to communicate. When you communicate, you share feelings and ideas with other people. When you communicate through art, you use a special kind of visual language.

In this unit, you will learn how artists plan their work by using **elements of design**. The elements

of design are part of the "language" of art. These elements are line, color, texture, value, space and shape.

You will also learn ways to combine visual elements by using principles of design. A **principle of design** is a guide for planning artworks that express ideas or feelings. Some principles of design are rhythm, balance, pattern and proportion. Others are emphasis, unity and variety.

What kinds of art do you see in pictures A, B and C? What elements and principles of design can you identify in each artwork? What messages do the artworks communicate?

C ***Effigy,*** Indonesia. Photograph: Ron Dahlquist, Superstock, Inc.

How Artists Work
Making Sketches

1

Théodore Géricault, *Sketches of a Wild Striped Cat,* 1812–1815. Pencil on paper, 12 5/8 x 15 3/4 " (32 x 40 cm). Réunion des Musées Nationaux. Photograph ©R.M.N.

The drawings in this lesson are sketches. A **sketch** is a drawing an artist makes for himself or herself. Sketches can be made for different reasons.

Sometimes artists make sketches to remember and understand what they see. An artist made the sketches in picture A over 150 years ago. These sketches of a cat show many expressions and positions of the animal.

Notice how the artist has observed the shape of the eyes, mouth and head. Why is each sketch slightly different from the others?

8   *Unit 1 Communicating Through Art*

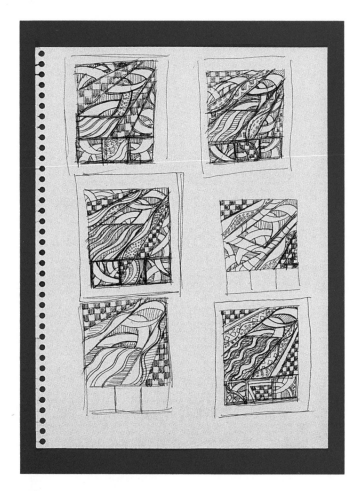

 B **Patricia A. Renick,** sketches for *Spectrum I,* 1991. Courtesy of the artist.

C **Patricia A. Renick,** *Spectrum I,* 1991. Acrylic on canvas, 38 x 46" (96 x 117 cm). Courtesy of the artist.

Artists also create sketches to help them think about ideas for artworks. In picture B, you see a page with six small sketches by artist Patricia A. Renick. She made these sketches to explore ideas for the painting in picture C.

Study the sketches and look at the painting. Can you tell which sketch she used to plan the painting?

Why are some parts of the painting different from the sketch?

Sketching is an activity you can do at home. You can sketch any time you have paper and a pen or pencil.

Your sketches for art lessons can help you to **design**, or plan, artworks such as paintings or sculptures. Your sketches can also help you learn to see and think about art.

Movement, Line and Shape
Creating Wordless Messages

 Dallas B. Taylor, *Cosmos,* 1985. Mixed media, 6 x 14" (15 x 35 cm). Courtesy of the artist.

From the time you are born, you see and feel motions. You remember the **motion** from rocking chairs, swings and slides. You remember the motion of bouncing balls, butterflies and swirls of water.

Memories like these help you see motion in artworks. In picture A, for example, the curved lines and shapes seem to swirl. They loop around and swing out into space. What other ideas about motion seem to go with the artwork?

Artists say that lines and shapes can send "wordless" messages or feelings to people. For example, **vertical** lines remind people of things that reach up. **Horizontal** lines remind people of calm, quiet feelings. What messages might people get from an artwork with many **diagonal** and zigzag lines? Why?

circle   oval   ellipse   curved free form

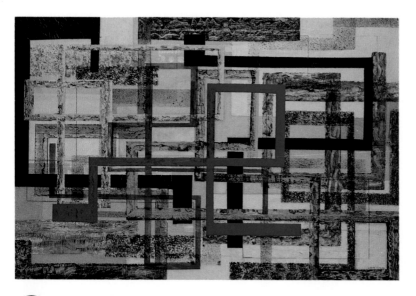

C **Irene Rice Pereira, *Daybreak.*** Oil on canvas, 40 x 60" (102 x 152 cm).
The Metropolitan Museum of Art, New York (The Edward Joseph
Gallagher III Memorial Collection, 1955).

E Student artwork.

What kind of motions or messages come from the artwork in picture C? Where do lines and shapes seem to move toward you? Where do lines and shapes seem to move away from you? Why? Look at the student artwork in picture E. Can you find similar motions? What are some differences in these two artworks?

Try this experiment. Create an artwork with curved lines and shapes (see picture B) or straight lines and shapes (see picture D). Draw several large shapes first. Add more shapes and lines to create a feeling of motion or another "wordless" message. Add colors that help to express the message.

D

square triangle rectangles angular
free form

11

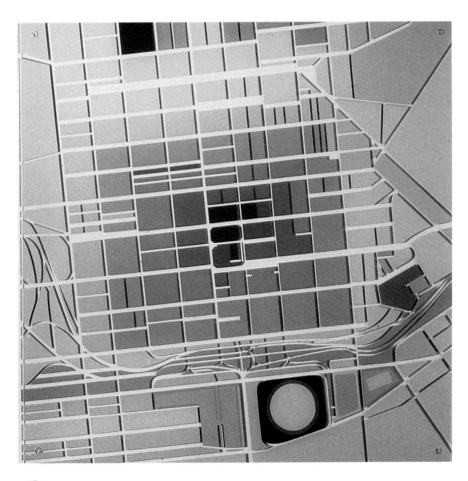

B

A **Judith Wittlin,** *Cincinnati,* 1982. Acrylic, acrylite, 30 x 30" (76 x 76 cm).
Courtesy of the artist.

Have you ever seen a view from the air in a movie or on television? A view of the earth from the sky is like a map with lines and shapes.

Look at Judith Wittlin's painting in picture A. It has design ideas that came from a map of Cincinnati, Ohio. Most of the lines and shapes in her painting are geometric. **Geometric** means the lines and shapes have smooth, even edges.

In most maps, geometric lines and shapes show where people have constructed roads and planned towns. Can you explain why geometric lines and shapes on a map usually show the **human-made environment**?

Artist Claude Breeze created the map-like painting in picture C. His design ideas came from a map of his hometown (see picture B).

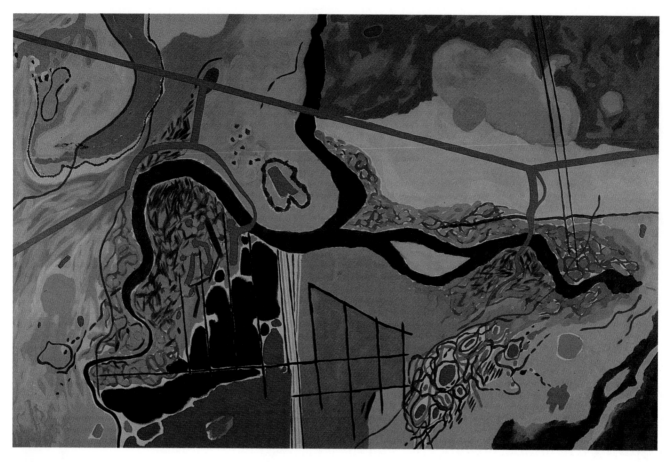

C

Claude Herbert Breeze, *Canadian Atlas: Position of London,* 1974. Acrylic on canvas, 67 x 102 1/2 " (170 x 260 cm). Government of Ontario Art Collection, Toronto. Photograph: Tom Moore Photography, Toronto.

Many of the lines and shapes in picture C have organic, or uneven, curves. **Organic** lines and shapes remind you of rivers, hills and other curved things in the **natural environment**. Most natural forms that move, live or change have irregular curves. Can you explain why?

Create an artwork that shows a map-like view of the land. You might imagine or recall views from an airplane. You might sketch a map that shows how you travel from home to school. Your ideas might come from studying maps of your city or state. You are making an original artwork. You are not copying or drawing over a map.

Remember that geometric lines and shapes usually show the roads and city blocks in the human-made environment. Organic lines and shapes usually show the natural environment.

13

A **Remy Duval, *Tree Near Arles.*** Photograph, 12 x 15 3/4" (30 x 40 cm). ©1984 Sotheby Parke Bernet, Inc.

B **Harry Callahan, *Chicago,*** 1950. Courtesy of Pace/MacGill Gallery, New York. Photograph ©Harry Callahan.

Almost everything you see has a main shape and many smaller shapes. Sometimes the main shape is similar to a **geometric** shape. Geometric shapes are shown in the center column of pictures C and E. Can you find similar shapes in your classroom?

Many shapes in your world are similar to geometric shapes. Even **natural shapes**, such as trees, can be similar to geometric shapes. For example, the tree top in picture A is like half of an oval or ellipse.

Many forms in nature also have a "skeleton" or **structure**. You can see the structure of a tree in the trunk and branches. Look at the photograph in picture B. Have you seen trees with structures like these?

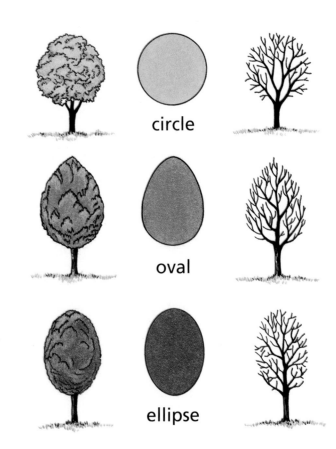

circle

oval

ellipse

C

D *Julie Bozzi, Frontage Road-Fort Worth, Texas,* 1982. Watercolor, 3 x 10" (8 x 24 cm). Courtesy of the artist.

In most trees the trunk is much thicker than the limbs. The limbs gradually get smaller as they grow upward and outward. Why is this structure so common in trees? Where do you find similar structures? Why?

Look at the painting in picture D. Can you see how the artist observed the main shapes of trees and bushes? Can you find some of the structures too?

Practice drawing trees and other things you see. Sketch the main shapes first. Then sketch the skeleton and smaller shapes. Add details, such as textures and leaves, last. These are steps many artists use for sketching. Can you explain why?

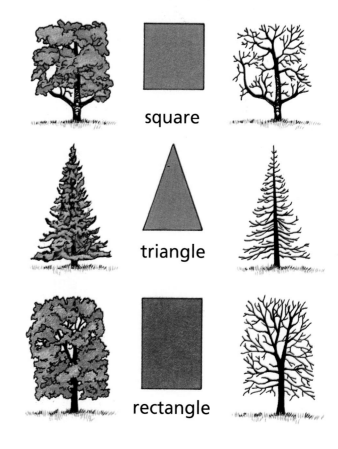

square

triangle

rectangle

E

5 Value and Texture
Seeing Light and Shadow

A

B

Georgia O'Keeffe, *Drawing IV*, 1959. Charcoal, 18 1/2 x 24 1/2" (47 x 62 cm). Collection of Whitney Museum of American Art, New York (Gift of Chauncy L. Wadell in honor of John I. H. Baur).

Artists study the light and the shadows on things they see. Light and shadows help us to know if an object is flat or round, smooth or rough.

Look at the photograph in picture A. Where are the lightest and darkest areas? Notice the gradual change from light to dark. How does this **shading** help you know the form is round?

Now look at the rough texture of the bark. The **texture** comes from small patches of shadow that you see on the bark. The shadows create a feeling of roughness.

Picture B shows a drawing of a tree. The artist has shaded the tree bark so it looks very smooth. She has also used very gradual changes in **value**, or light and dark, to make the forms look round.

The source of light is on the left. The shadows are on the right. What happens when the position of the light changes?

C

Artists invent ways to suggest forms and textures in drawings. The five trees in picture C are shaded in different ways. Which trees are shaded to create a smooth texture? Why are all of the trees darker on one side and lighter on the other?

Try different ways to draw and shade objects so the forms show up. Experiment with ways to suggest textures. A student made the drawing in picture D. How did she draw forms and textures?

D   Student artwork.

17

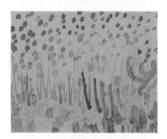

A   Vincent van Gogh, *View of Arles*, 1888. Ink, 17 11/16 x 21 5/8" (45 x 55 cm). Museum of Art, Rhode Island School of Design (Gift of Mrs. Murray S. Danforth). Photograph: Cathy Carver.

B   Vincent van Gogh, *View of Arles* (three details).

When you hold a rock or a stick, you are touching a surface that has textures. Textures can feel rough, smooth, gritty or fluffy. They can feel shaggy or silky. Textures that you can feel by touch are called **tactile textures**.

You can also identify textures just by seeing them. **Visual textures** are patterns of light and shadow.

Look at the drawing in picture A. Small patterns of lines help you see the textures of tall and short plants in the field. How did the artist show the textures of trees?

This drawing was made with pen and ink. In picture B, you see some of the marks the artist made with the pen. Marks like these are called **invented textures**.

 Deborah Morrissey McGoff, *Florida Palmetto Series #5,* 1982. Oil pastel, 13 1/4 x 16 " (34 x 41 cm). Courtesy of the artist.

 Deborah Morrissey McGoff, *Florida Palmetto Series #5* (detail).

You can also suggest textures by shading. The drawing in picture C has **shading**, or very gradual changes in light and dark areas. The shading helps you see the textures of the sand and bushes.

This artist also suggests textures by using colors. Look at the large green bushes. They are not one color of green. The artist used yellow-green, blue-green and other colors related to green. Why do these changes in green help to show textures? What changes in color help to show the texture of sand?

Choose a medium for drawing that you like to use. Sketch some ideas for a real or imaginary landscape. Try ways to show textures in the landscape. Use your best ideas to create your drawing.

19

Texture in Different Media
Creating Monoprints

Edgar Degas, *The Jet Earring,* ca.1877–1880.
Monoprint, 3 3/16 x 2 3/4" (8 x 7 cm).
The Metropolitan Museum of Art, New York
(Anonymous Gift in memory of Francis Henry
Taylor, 1959).

Edgar Degas created artworks that show people in unusual views. What view do you see in picture A? Notice the texture of the hair. The artist does not show every tiny hair. He suggests the flowing hairstyle. How does he show the hat and its feathers?

Edgar Degas was interested in capturing a quick impression of people. An impression is a picture or idea that lacks detail. This art style is called **Impressionism**. Edgar Degas and other artists in France explored this style.

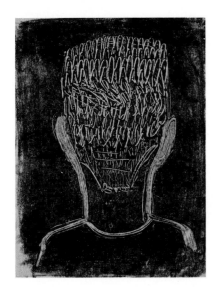

B

The artworks in this lesson are **monoprints**. To create a monoprint, put ink or paint on a smooth surface like plastic or metal. Then wipe away some of the ink to create lines, shapes and textures. To make a print of the picture, put paper over the whole design. Rub the paper to press the ink onto it. Some of the tools and materials for monoprinting are shown in picture C.

Students created the monoprints in picture B. They used different tools to create the feeling of texture in hair and the fur of animals. What tools do you think they used?

Experiment with monoprinting. Then create a monoprint that includes a very unusual view and textures.

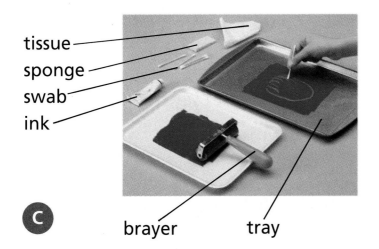

tissue
sponge
swab
ink

C

brayer　　tray

"Pulling" the print.

21

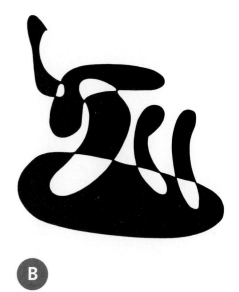

 Joan Miró, *Painting*, 1933. Oil on canvas, 68 1/2 x 83 1/4" (174 x 211 cm). Collection, The Museum of Modern Art, New York (Loula D. Lasker Bequest).

Many artists like to create designs that have unusual combinations of shapes. The artwork in picture A is filled with shapes that **overlap**. The shapes seem to float in space. The light and dark colors create a puzzle-like pattern of shapes.

Can you see how the artist painted the overlapping shapes? Look for edges of shapes where the colors change. Shapes that go across each other have been colored in (see picture B).

In pictures A and B, most people see the dark shapes first. These shapes are called positive shapes. A **positive shape** stands out from the background. It has edges or colors that get your attention quickly.

You see **negative shapes** around or between the positive shapes. The positive and negative shapes in this artwork are equally important. They help you discover new shapes next to others.

Josef Albers, *Aquarium,* 1934. Woodcut, 7 1/8 x 10 1/4" (18 x 26 cm). Philadelphia Museum of Art (Print Club, Permanent Collection).

D

C

Courtesy of Taylor & Browning Design Associates, Toronto.

Packages and signs often have designs with positive and negative shapes. How did the designer of the shopping bag use positive and negative shapes?

Look at the artwork in picture D. The artist drew a looping line. Then he planned the design so the black and white shapes are side by side. Can you point to the positive and negative shapes?

Look for other examples of designs with positive and negative shapes. You can find some examples in this book. You can find others in magazines, signs and packages.

See if you can create a puzzle-like artwork using positive and negative shapes.

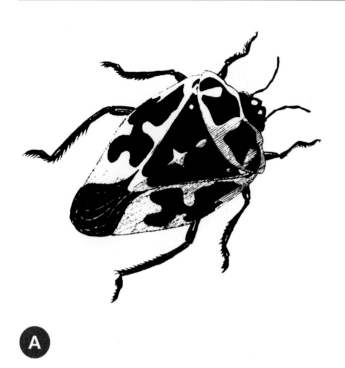

A

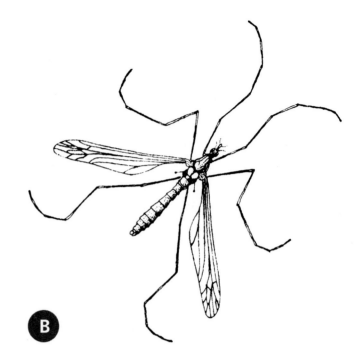

B

C

Many artists like to study nature. They look for lines and shapes in plants, animals and other living things. Artists study the textures, patterns and design of many things.

Study these insects as an artist might. Look for different kinds of lines. Is the body of each insect the same shape? What patterns do you see?

Now look at the **views** and arrangements of parts of the insects. Seven of the insects are shown from the top view. The top view shows the symmetry of the body, wings and other parts. **Symmetry** means that one half is like the other half.

One insect is shown from a side view. Can you find it? Notice that the left and right half of the insect do not look alike. In this side view, you see the **asymmetry** of the body. If you could see the other insects from a side view, they would also look asymmetrical. Can you explain why?

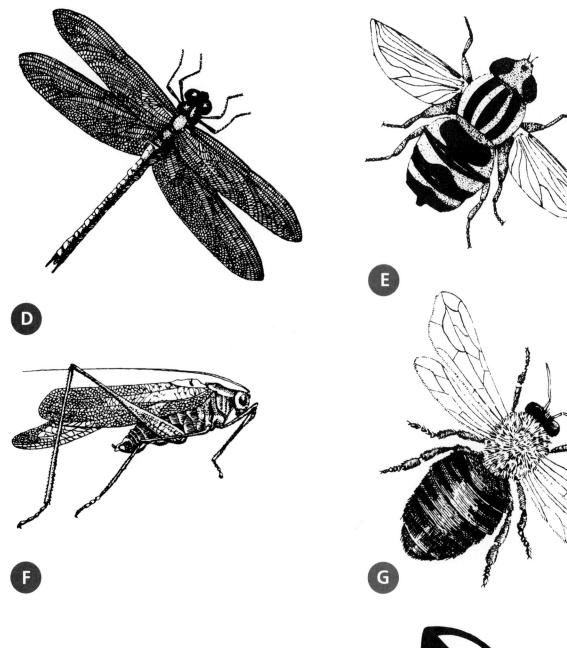

D

E

F

G

Draw a real or imaginary insect. Draw the top view or the side view. Make your drawing very dark. Your drawing should have thick lines and simple shapes. You will use your drawing in the next lesson to create a print.

H

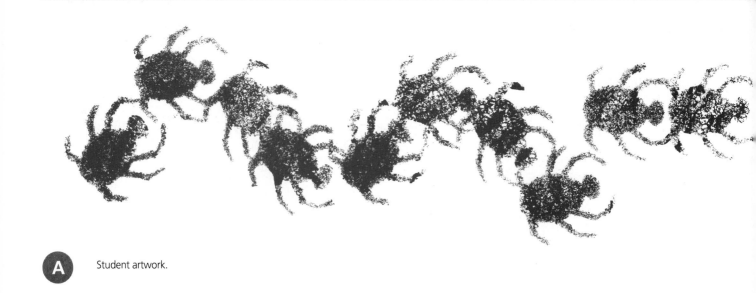

A Student artwork.

A student in Indiana made this **print** from a stencil. Her print shows the motion of a crawling insect.

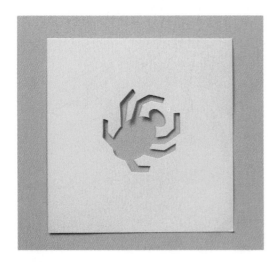

B

C

Picture B is a **stencil** cut from paper. The holes in this stencil made a good print. The shapes and lines of the insect are wide and open.

Place your stencil on paper. Hold the stencil. Gently press paint through the holes. Carefully lift the stencil. The painted shape is a stencil print.

You can show motion by printing your stencil many times. Print some light colors first. Then print darker colors on top of the light colors. What are some other ways to suggest **motion** in your print?

The stencil print in picture D was made by an Inuit artist who lives in Canada, on Baffin Island. The print illustrates the myth of Sedna, a spirit who lives in the sea. Sedna provides food to people and protects animals. How did the artist show motion?

 Ananaisee Alikatuktuk, *Talleelayu and Family,* 1976. Stencil print, 15 3/8 x 23 1/4" (39 x 59 cm). Canadian Museum of Civilization.

11

Line and Movement
Sketching People in Action

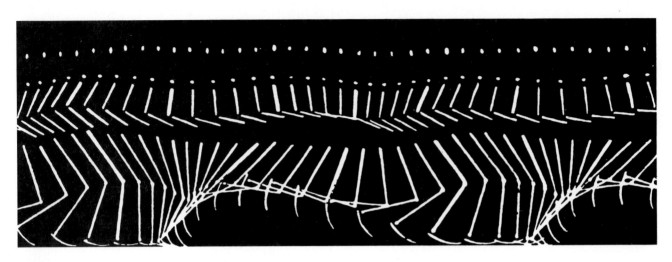

 Jules-Étienne Marey, *Study of Man Walking*. From *Le Nature,* September 29, 1883.

What part of your body can move in a circle? Can you bend your body to create diagonal lines? The photograph in picture A was created by attaching lights to a person and recording the motion. Can you see what the person was doing?

You can learn to draw people in different **poses**. Practice will help you draw people who are dancing, playing or sitting quietly.

 Photograph: Fred Fehl.

 Norman Rockwell, *Football Player*.
Photograph ©1979 by Famous Artists School.

The boy in picture B posed for Norman Rockwell's drawing. Can you find a similar pose in picture D? How can you tell that the dancer in picture C is moving her body?

Norman Rockwell, *First Down.* Art from the Archives of Brown and Bigelow.

Many artists practice drawing people. Norman Rockwell drew this illustration for a magazine. The artist often asked people to pose so that he could sketch them. A person who poses for an artist is called a **model**.

Today you will practice drawing students in your class. Some students will be models. They will pose so that everyone can practice drawing.

Jacob Lawrence, *Parade,* 1960. Tempera with pencil underdrawing on fiberboard, 23 7/8 x 30 1/8" (61 x 77 cm). Hirshhorn Museum and Sculpture Garden, Smithsonian Institution, Washington, DC (Gift of Joseph H. Hirshhorn, 1966). Photograph: Lee Stalsworth.

Jacob Lawrence is a well-known African-American artist. His painting in picture A has several visual rhythms. A **visual rhythm** is created by repeating lines, shapes and colors. How is a visual rhythm like a rhythm in music or dance? How is it different?

Visual rhythms can come from shapes that overlap. **Overlap** means that some shapes are in front of others (see picture B).

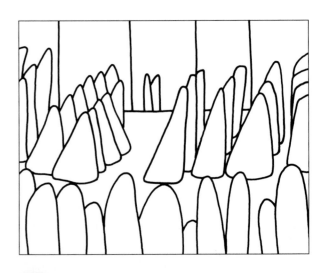

 Shiavax Chavda, *Naga Dancers,* 1954. Watercolor, 7 1/2 x 12 " (19 x 30 cm). Private Collection.

The artist who created the painting in picture C was born in India. The dancers are overlapped to create a visual rhythm. Curved and wavy lines create a visual rhythm across the painting.

Visual rhythms help to express a feeling of **motion**. The artwork in picture A has many diagonal lines to express a marching rhythm. What kind of rhythm do you see and feel from the design in picture C?

Draw a crowd of people in costumes or uniforms. Show the people overlapping each other. Begin by drawing a few people quite large. Then draw other people behind the first ones. Repeat shapes and colors so that your picture has some visual rhythms.

What objects in these paintings can you name? Why do you think the artists chose these objects for a painting?

An artwork that shows objects is a **still life**. The paintings of still life in this lesson are planned so that you see the design elements. The textures, spaces and patterns are especially important.

 A Margaret Burroughs, *Still Life,* ca. 1943. Oil on canvas, 19 1/2 x 15 1/2 " (50 x 39 cm). Evans-Tibbs Gallery, Washington, DC.

Many still lifes are planned so the shapes overlap. Can you find some of the overlapping shapes in both of these still lifes?

The shapes are also grouped so that your eyes move from the **foreground** to the **middleground** and then to the **background**. These three divisions of **space** help to make shapes look near to you or far away. Can you find the foreground, middleground and background in both paintings?

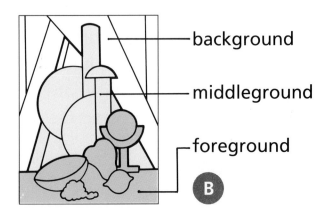

background

middleground

foreground

B

Both of these paintings have many invented patterns and textures. These invented elements give the paintings an abstract style. **Abstract** means the artist has added or changed parts. The artwork does not look realistic.

Albert Dumouchel, *Still Life,* 1946. Oil on panel, 30 5/16 x 25 5/8" (77 x 65 cm). Collection of the National Bank of Canada, Montreal.

With help from your teacher and classmates, collect some objects and set up several still lifes. One still life might have sports equipment. Another still life might have musical instruments. What are some other ideas for still lifes? Try to arrange the objects so that they overlap and create a well-planned design.

Choose one of the still lifes to draw. Draw the **contours,** or edges, of all the shapes. Show how the shapes overlap.

Fill the picture with invented textures and patterns. Repeat some of the colors, lines and shapes. Repetition will give unity to your still life. The invented textures and patterns will make your painting look abstract.

Color Relationships
Mixing Colors of Paint

Many artists have created paintings of flowers in a vase. This still life painting is by African-American artist Laura Wheeler Waring. The very dark background **contrasts** with the bright colors of the flowers.

Each flower in this painting has several related colors. The large red flower, for example, has some orange and red-orange in it. **Related colors** are next to each other on the color wheel in picture B. You can learn to mix and use related colors in paintings.

 Laura Wheeler Waring, *Still Life,* 1928. Oil on canvas. Evans-Tibbs Gallery, Washington, DC.

Let's review some ideas about mixing colors of paint. The name of a color is its **hue**. The common hues are rainbow colors: red, yellow, orange, green, blue and violet. Picture B shows these "rainbow" hues arranged in a circle.

You can mix many colors from the three **primary colors**: red, yellow and blue. If you mix red and yellow, you get orange. What colors do you mix to get green and violet? Orange, green and violet are called **secondary colors**.

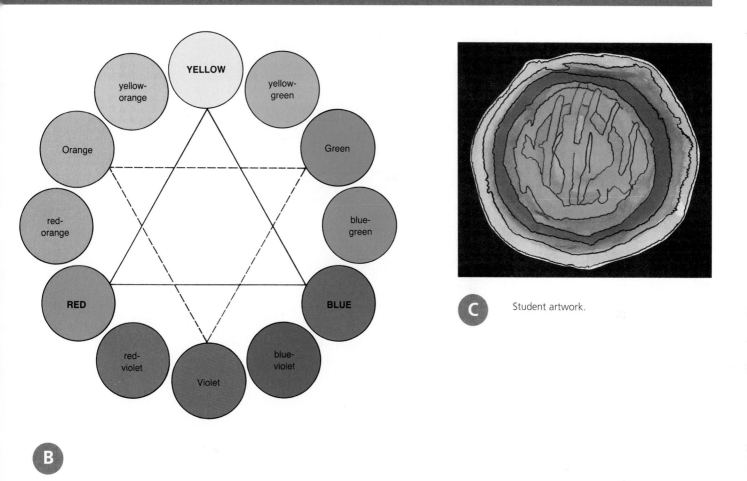

YELLOW

yellow-orange

yellow-green

Orange

Green

red-orange

blue-green

RED

BLUE

red-violet

blue-violet

Violet

B

C Student artwork.

Now look at the **intermediate colors** on the color wheel. They have names like blue-violet and blue-green. What are the other intermediate colors? How do you think these are mixed?

Create a painting that has many related colors. Your painting might be a realistic still life or an abstract artwork. A student created the abstract artwork in picture C.

You may want to mount your work on a dark, contrasting background paper to make colors look very bright. What other ideas can you explore?

Remember that related colors are next to each other on the color wheel. It is usually best to mix and apply the lightest colors first. Can you explain why?

Abstract and Realistic Art
Painting a Still Life

Artists have their own **styles** of painting. You can see these differences in the two still life paintings in this lesson. Both paintings show objects on display in a market. One painting has an abstract style. The other has a realistic style.

 Amelia Peláez del Casal, *Fishes,* 1943. Oil on canvas, 45 1/2 x 35 1/8" (116 x 89 cm). Collection, The Museum of Modern Art, New York (Inter-American Fund).

Fishes is an abstract painting. **Abstract** means the artist has invented shapes, colors and lines instead of trying to paint a likeness. This painting has many shapes and colors that fit together like a puzzle. Dark lines create patterns. Many shapes are outlined in dark colors.

Imagine you were the artist who created this painting. Would you draw some of the main shapes before you mixed paints? Why or why not? What colors of paint would you mix and apply first? Why? What parts would you paint last? Why?

B Gustave Caillebotte, *Fruit Displayed on a Stand,* ca. 1881–1882. Oil on canvas, 30 1/8 x 39 5/8"
(77 x 101 cm). Museum of Fine Arts, Boston (Fannie P. Mason Fund in Memory of Alice Thevin).

Can you imagine how picture B was painted? Most likely, the artist painted the lightest shapes first. Then the artist probably mixed colors for the shadows. Shadows help to make an artwork look **realistic**. What colors are used for shading the white paper around the fruit? What colors make the yellow fruit look round? What else makes this painting look more realistic than *Fishes*?

You have many choices when you create a painting. You can choose which colors to put down first. You can think about the brushstrokes you will use. You can decide if you will blend colors or keep them separated. When you make choices like this, you are deciding the style of your painting.

A   **Charles Burchfield, *East Wind and Winter Sun*.** Watercolor, 29 5/8 x 39 1/2" (75 x 100 cm). The Baltimore Museum of Art (Edward Joseph Gallagher III Memorial Collection).

In this unit, you have learned about some of the **elements and principles of design**. Use what you have learned to analyze the design in each painting. **Analyze** means seeing and thinking about the parts and how they work together.

Each artist has expressed different feelings and ideas about winter. The painting in picture A has a large sky filled with diagonal lines and curves. Why do these elements create a feeling of motion? What colors and brushstrokes help to express the feeling of a windy day? What other design elements and principles can you identify?

Marc-Aurèle de Foy Suzor-Coté, *Settlement on the Hillside,* 1909. Oil on canvas, 23 x 28 3/4" (58 x 73 cm). The National Gallery of Canada, Ottawa.

What design elements and principles do you see in picture B? For example, what fills most of the space? How does the artist show things that are near and far away? What colors help to show the snow and cold weather? What else can you describe and analyze?

Which painting looks calm, quiet and very cold? Which one looks full of motion, energy and some bright sunlight? What are some style names for each painting?

With your classmates, choose a season of the year. Create an artwork about the season in your own style. Make design choices that are very different from every other student's.

Georgia O'Keeffe, *The Mountain, New Mexico,* 1931. Oil on canvas, 30 x 36" (76 x 91 cm).
Collection of Whitney Museum of American Art, New York (Purchase).

In this unit, you will explore different subjects and themes in art. You will also learn more about design and styles of art. Both of these paintings are landscapes. A **landscape** is an artwork with an outdoor scene as the main subject. Both of these paintings also show mountains. Why do the paintings look very different?

The painting in picture A glows with many kinds of red, yellow and orange. The artist has used many **warm colors** to show the hot, dry mountains. What else did the artist want you to see and think about?

Ernst L. Kirchner, *Mountain Landscape from Clavadel.* Oil on canvas, 53 1/8 x 78 7/8" (135 x 201 cm). The Museum of Fine Arts, Boston (Tompkins Collection).

The painting in picture B has many kinds of blue, green and violet. These **cool colors** show the meadow, forest and mountains. Why do you think the artist used cool colors for this painting?

Warm and cool colors can show different places and things. They can also give you different moods or feelings. What special moods or feelings does each painting give you?

Think about places you have seen. You might imagine a place no one has been, such as a planet in space. Make some sketches of the landscape.

Choose warm or cool colors for your artwork. Create a definite mood or feeling by using many kinds of warm colors or many kinds of cool colors.

Using Watercolors
Painting About Moods

 Morris Louis, *Point of Tranquillity,* 1959–60. Synthetic polymer on canvas, 102 x 138" (258 x 343 cm). Hirshhorn Museum and Sculpture Garden, Smithsonian Institution, Washington, DC (Gift of Joseph H. Hirshhorn, 1966). Photograph: Lee Stalsworth.

Have you ever seen colors, shapes or lines that gave you a special feeling? The two paintings in this lesson are abstract artworks. They have themes that express feelings. Sometimes this style is called **Abstract Expressionism**.

Look at *Point of Tranquillity* by Morris Louis. The paint flows outward and inward at the same time. The colors blend and flow together. Tranquility means being peaceful, quiet and calm.

Now look at the painting in picture B by Alma Thomas. Do you see the flowing, watery effect in the paint? Why do you think the colors are dark and blurry? What does the title tell you?

These artists have used thin, or **diluted**, paint to express ideas and feelings. The thin paint looks transparent. **Transparent** means that white or another color shows underneath the paint.

 Alma Thomas, *Leaves Outside a Window in Rain,* 1966. Watercolor. Evans-Tibbs Gallery, Washington, DC.

You can use diluted tempera or transparent **watercolor paints** to express ideas and feelings. Watercolors are usually in small pans inside of a box. The lid of the box is a **palette**, or small mixing tray.

Begin your painting on damp paper. Brush some light colors on the paper. Let ideas come to you from the way the colors flow together. Gradually add darker colors. As your painting begins to dry, add details. Wash, wipe and blot your brush when you change colors. Can you explain why?

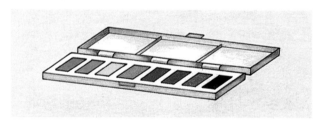

watercolor paints

wash   wipe   blot

C

Mixing Tints and Shades
Paintings About the Sea

Milton Avery, *Boats in Yellow Sea,* 1944. Gouache on paper, 22 x 30" (56 x 76 cm). Edwin A. Ulrich Museum of Art, The Wichita State University (Endowment Association Art Collection).

Many artists have created paintings about the sea, ocean and large lakes. Artworks that show a large body of water are called **seascapes**. The artworks in this lesson show some ways artists use values, or light and dark colors.

Most of the colors in Milton Avery's seascape are tints. A **tint** is a light value of a color. You mix a tint by adding white to a color. What tints do you see in this painting? How did the artist mix them?

Why might the artist use so many tints, or light values, in this painting? Do these colors make you think of a special time of day? Do they give you ideas about the weather? What other feelings or ideas do the colors give you? How else does the artist send you messages?

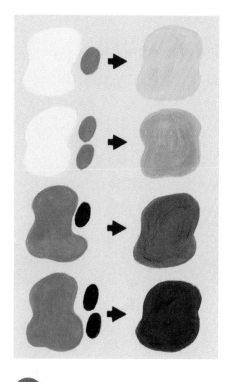

C

B **Raoul Dufy,** *Regatta at Cowes,* 1934. Oil on linen canvas, 32 1/8 x 39 1/2 " (82 x 100 cm).
National Gallery of Art, Washington, DC (Ailsa Mellon Bruce Collection).

Do you see many boats with flags in picture B? This painting was created by Raoul Dufy. A regatta is a festive boat race.

How does the artist capture the idea and feeling of a "festival" of boats? How does he suggest that the water and boats are moving?

Regatta is filled with many values of blue. Can you find some dark values, or shades? A **shade** is mixed by adding black to a color. Why has the artist used many tints and shades of blue? What other colors do you see?

Think about a real or imaginary seascape that you could show in a painting. It could be full of action or very calm. What colors will you use? How can you mix them?

D

Student artwork.

45

Using Color Schemes
Sparkling Landscapes

Artists can create bright, sparkling paintings by planning their colors. A plan for using colors is a **color scheme**. The color wheel can help you understand some ways of planning colors.

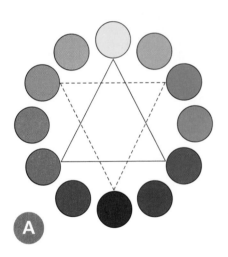

A

B Claude Monet, *Meadow at Giverny,* 19th century. Oil on canvas, 36 1/4 x 32 1/8" (92 x 82 cm). Museum of Fine Arts, Boston (Juliana Cheney Edwards Collection).

The painting in picture B is planned around a related, or analogous, color scheme. **Analogous** colors are next to each other on the color wheel. Yellow-orange, yellow and yellow-green are related colors. Look at the color wheel. Can you find other sets of analogous colors on the color wheel?

Claude Monet used analogous colors in picture B. The colors seem to blend and sparkle in this scene.

His style of painting is called **Impressionism**. When you look at something quickly, you get an impression of it. Artists who work in this style want to show a scene quickly, before the light and color change.

D Student artwork.

C **Howard Storm,** *Burning Bush,* 1981. Oil on canvas, 28 x 22" (71 x 56 cm). Courtesy of the artist.

Look at Howard Storm's painting in picture C. It has a complementary color scheme. **Complementary colors** are opposite from each other on the color wheel. These colors create strong contrasts that get your attention.

Can you find complementary colors on the color wheel? What are the complementary colors in Howard Storm's painting? What kind of light do the colors help him to show?

Most artists who work in the Impressionist style make sketches or paintings outdoors. They observe colors but they also use colors inventively. For example, these artists rarely use black for shadows. They use colors like bluish black, dark green or dark red.

Make some sketches outdoors on a sunny day. Sketch the scene using analogous or complementary colors. Then create an artwork based on your sketches. What color schemes do you see in the student art in picture D?

47

 Joseph Stella, *Battle of Lights, Coney Island,* 1913–14. Oil on canvas, 75 3/4 x 34" (192 x 89 cm). Yale University Art Gallery (Gift of Collection Société Anonyme).

Have you ever been to an amusement park? Have you ever seen the swirling, sparkling lights of a fair or festival? How can you capture the feeling of crowds, action and excitement in a big city?

The two paintings in this lesson suggest energy and excitement. The paintings do not show a realistic scene. They are **abstract** artworks.

Both of these paintings are planned around "action" lines and shapes. Some of these lines and shapes are shown in pictures B and D. Can you see similar lines and shapes in each painting?

 B

Joaquín Torres-García, *New York City: Bird's-Eye View,* ca.1920. Gouache on cardboard, 13 5/16 x 19 1/8" (34 x 49 cm). Yale University Art Gallery (Gift of Collection Société Anonyme).

Action lines help to lead your eyes through the space of the whole picture. They give unity to the variety of colors, patterns and details. **Unity** means that visual elements are working together, like a team.

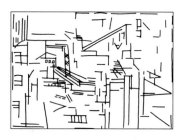

Think of very busy, exciting places you have been. Think about the "action" lines and shapes that go with the activity. The lines and shapes may be choppy, zig-zaggy or graceful.

Draw your action lines on paper to give unity to the design. Then add colors, patterns and other details to your work. Create an abstract artwork filled with action and excitement.

Imagining the Impossible
Drawing Mechanimals

A   **Murray Tinkelman, *Mechanimal*,** 1978. Courtesy of the artist.

Imagination helps you think about things in a new or different way. There are many ways to use your imagination for artwork.

You can combine ideas that seem to be very different. That is one way to use your imagination. What ideas did the artist, Murray Tinkelman, combine in his two drawings of "mechanimals?"

How are machines and animals different? Can you think of ways that animals and machines might be alike?

B   **Murray Tinkelman, *Mechanimal*,** 1978. Courtesy of the artist.

Wanda Gag, *Stone Crusher,* 1929. Lithograph, 14 3/8 x 11 3/8" (37 x 29 cm).
Philadelphia Museum of Art (Harrison Fund).

See if you can create a drawing of a "mechanimal." Use your imagination. Create an original drawing. Original art is your own work. It is not copied.

There are many ways to use your imagination for art. Study this picture by artist Wanda Gag. Do you think she used her imagination? How?

 Patricia A. Renick, maquette for ***Stegowagenvolkssaurus.***
Courtesy of the artist.

 B

Men and women who create art learn to work hard. They learn to design and plan what they make. They learn to look at their world and to use their imagination. You are learning to do these things too.

The sculpture in picture D was created by Patricia Renick. She built the sculpture around the body of a real car. Some of the parts are made of Fiberglas. The artist made the Fiberglas parts in a factory.

The artist's first idea for this artwork is shown in picture A. She added oil-based clay to a toy car. This kind of small model is often used to plan a very large sculpture. Can you explain why?

 C

In picture B, you see the real car. It is held up by an **armature**, or support, made of steel. The artist glued Styrofoam to the armature and car. In picture C, you see the artist adding clay and carving it. The clay was covered with Fiberglas® to create the final work in picture D.

Patricia Renick worked on this sculpture every day for a year. Imagine that you are helping her build the sculpture. It is 12 feet tall (3.7 m) and 20 feet long (6.1 m). The title is *Stegowagenvolkssaurus*.

Use your own imagination. What kind of imaginary creature can you create?

22

Using Color for Emphasis
Feelings About Animals

 Everett Spruce, *Big Turtle*. Oil on prestwood, 20 x 24" (51 x 61 cm). Wichita Art Museum, Wichita, Kansas (The Roland P. Murdock Collection). Photograph: Henry Nelson.

Have you ever had a very happy, scary or strange feeling about an animal? Artists who want to share a strong feeling often work in a style known as **Expressionism**. The paintings in this lesson are examples of this style of art.

Notice how the shapes of the animals fill most of the space. The animals are the **center of interest**. In many Expressionist artworks, some design elements are given more importance, or **emphasis**, than others.

Franz Marc, *The Yellow Cow,* 1911. Oil on canvas, 55 3/8 x 74 1/2 " (141 x 189 cm). Photograph: David Heald. Photograph ©The Solomon R. Guggenheim Foundation, New York.

Student artwork.

In picture A, you see very strong textures. There are very few curves. Most of the lines and shapes are angular. Why do you think the artist chose to emphasize these design elements? What feelings do they help to capture?

In picture B, the artist has used many curved lines and shapes. The painting is filled with **complementary colors** such as yellow and violet, red and green. What feelings do you get from these strong, contrasting colors?

A student from a village in India created the painting in picture C. It expresses a feeling of surprise when she and a baby tiger saw each other.

Think of a real or imaginary animal and your feelings about it. Make sketches to try out ideas for the view and the size of the animal. Explore ideas for colors and textures.

Choose your best sketch and create an expressive drawing or painting. You might combine media such as paint, crayon and markers.

Centers of Interest
A Relief Print of Animals

A **Wanda Gag,** *Cats at Window,* 1930. Wood engraving, comp: 2 15/16 x 3 13/16 " (7 x 10 cm); sheet: 3 1/2 x 7 1/2 " (9 x 19 cm). Philadelphia Museum of Art (Thomas Skelton Harrison Fund).

The artwork in picture A is a **print**. To make the print, the artist carved a picture in a smooth **block** of wood. She put thick ink on the wood and pressed the paper against the ink. She made many prints in this way.

What are the main centers of interest in this print? How does the artist lead your eyes toward these areas? What is the theme in this work?

Look again at the print in picture A. How did the artist create the feeling of texture in the cats' fur? Where else do you see textures or small patterns? How did the artist show the window and curtains?

There are many ways to make prints. Some prints are made by carving lines and shapes into wood or metal. Artists often draw their design or picture on paper before they carve it.

A student made the printing block in picture B. He pressed lines, shapes and textures into a block of Styrofoam. He drew the pictures and the letters backwards. He reversed them so that the final print would look right.

B

Plan the drawing for your print on thin paper. If you turn the paper over, you can see the reversed image. Trace this reversed image on your block.

Make some prints. Press your design into a block of Styrofoam. Then follow the other steps in picture D.

Keep your best prints. After they are dry, put your name and a title on your prints.

C

Student artwork.

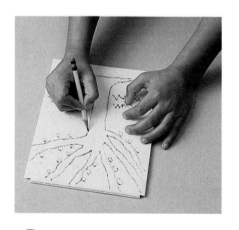  

D

After you prepare your block, put ink or paint on it. A **brayer** is a roller artists use to apply ink.

Put paper on top of the inked block. Rub the back of the paper gently. Lift the paper carefully.

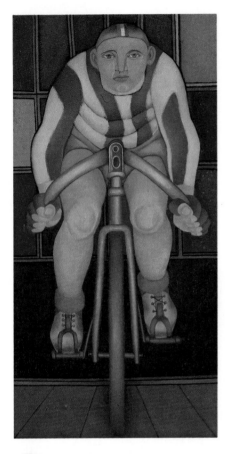

A

Richard Lindner, *Cyclist,* 1951.
24 1/2 x 12 " (62 x 30 cm).
Kunsthalle, Germany.

C

Jean Metzinger, *At the Cycle-Race Track,* ca. 1914. Oil and
collage on canvas, 51 3/8 x 38 1/4 " (130 x 97 cm). The Solomon
R. Guggenheim Foundation, New York (Peggy Guggenheim
Collection, Venice). Photograph: David Heald. Photograph
©The Solomon R. Guggenheim Foundation, New York.

Every day you see many views of
people, places and objects. A **view** is
the position of something when you
look at it. The shapes and lines of
objects look different in each view
you see.

Picture A is a painting that shows
the front view of a bicycle and a rider.
How did the artist show the parts of
the bicycle and rider?

The painting in picture C shows
one bicycle rider. What is unusual
about the view that you see? How
can you tell the rider is moving fast?
Which wheels look most like a true
circle, or the side view of a wheel?
Why? What views do you see in the
photographs of a rider in picture B?

Andrew Wyeth, *Young America,* 1950. Egg tempera on gessoed board, 32 1/2 x 45 1/4" (82 x 115 cm). Courtesy of The Pennsylvania Academy of the Fine Arts, Philadelphia (Joseph E. Temple Fund).

Picture D shows another painting with a bicycle rider. How does this view differ from the views in B?

Look again at the paintings and photographs. How does the human figure bend, sit and use the pedals on a bicycle? Why do these bends look different in each view?

Do you ride a bicycle? What are some other forms of transportation? Are there some unusual ways of traveling that you would like to try?

Imagine you could travel to school any way that you wished. Draw a picture of yourself using that kind of transportation. What view will you draw?

25 *Seeing Proportions* *Drawing Portraits*

A

Portrait of Chief Minister Mun Suk-Kong, 19th century, Yi Dynasty, Korea. Hanging scroll painting, ink and color on silk, 28 1/2 x 20 1/4" (72 x 51 cm). The Brooklyn Museum, New York (Gift of Dr. & Mrs. John Lyden).

B

Gustavo Lazarini, ***Aunt Juliana,*** 1941. Watercolor, 19 1/4 x 13 1/8" (49 x 33 cm). Collection, The Museum of Modern Art, New York (Inter-American Fund).

Today you will practice drawing the head and face of a person. Your drawing could be a portrait. A **portrait** is a likeness of a real person. It shows how a person looks or feels.

An unknown artist from Korea created the portrait in picture A. The man is dressed to show he was an important person. Where have you seen portraits of famous people?

An artist from South America created the portrait in picture B. The portrait shows his aunt. How does the artist help you see that she is very old? Why do many people want portraits of relatives or friends?

Some artists draw people to express a theme. The drawing in picture C shows a family. Does the title of the artwork help you interpret it?

C

1. Fold your paper. The folds will be guidelines for drawing.

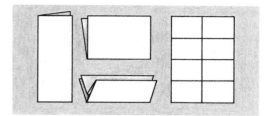

2. Observe and draw the shape of the head. Leave space near the edge of the paper to add the ears, hair and neck.

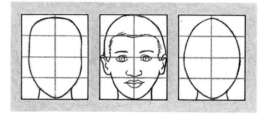

3. Draw the eyes, nose and other features near your guidelines. Look closely at the person and draw the shapes and details you see.

Study the instructions in picture D. The **guidelines** can help you see and draw proportions in a head. **Proportions** show how parts are related to each other. For example, the eyes are about halfway between the top of the head and the chin.

D Student artwork.

A portrait is an artwork that shows the likeness of a person. The paintings in this lesson are portraits of people in an environment. Each artist has also shown more than one person.

Portraits can be painted in different styles. The artist who created picture A was a leader of the **Expressionist** style. In this style, artists may use some colors as **symbols** for ideas and feelings.

For example, in this painting the eyes are a surprising green. Green is a symbol for growth and growing up. The boy and girl are also shown in a forest-like place where they see green things.

 Paula Modersohn-Becker, *Girl and Boy,* ca. 1903. Oil on cardboard, 21 1/2 x 13 5/8" (56 x 35 cm). The St. Louis Art Museum (Bequest of Morton D. May).

What else do you see? Do you see how shapes overlap each other? What shapes are in the foreground, or nearest to you? What does the background show? The boy is in the middleground, or the space between the foreground and the background.

The artwork in picture B is in a style called **Realism**. In this style, the artist creates the illusion that you are looking at a real scene.

The artist shows the **profile**, or side view, of a husband and wife. There are also portraits of children. How has the artist created the illusion of a real scene?

What do you see in the foreground? Where do you see shapes that overlap? What do you see in the background? What are some other ways to study these paintings?

B **Allan Rohan Crite,** *Harriet and Leon,* 1941. Oil on canvas, 35 x 30" (89 x 76 cm). The Boston Athenaeum (Gift of the artist).

Sketch people you know. Ask them to pose while you draw them. Plan a drawing or painting that shows these people in an environment. Draw the people large and plan the spaces around them.

If you create a painting, think about the steps you will use to mix and apply paint. For example, will you paint the background or foreground first? Why? Will you paint large shapes or details first? How can you decide?

63

 A

B Honoré Daumier, *They Say that the Parisians Are Difficult to Please, On these Four Benches Is Not one Discontent -- It Is True that All these Frenchmen are Romans,* 1864. Lithograph, 9 3/4 x 9 1/8 " (25 x 23 cm). Museum of Fine Arts, Boston (William P. Babcock Bequest,1992).

You can learn to draw crowds quickly, just as artists learn to do. Draw several people large, near the bottom of your paper. These people will be in the **foreground** of your picture.

Then draw other people behind the first ones you drew. Draw them smaller and above the first people you drew. Add more people in the same way. All of the people in the **background** should be drawn smaller.

The drawing in picture B was created more than 100 years ago by a French artist, Honoré Daumier. He created many drawings that were **editorial cartoons** in newspapers.

How could Honoré Daumier quickly draw so many people? Are the heads of all the people the same size? Why or why not? Look at the people in the foreground. Why are they shown with more details than people in the background?

 José Clemente Orozco, *Zapatistas,* 1936. Lithograph, 13 x 16 1/2" (33 x 42 cm). Private Collection.

The drawing in picture C was created by José Clemente Orozco. This Mexican artist believed his people needed new leaders to become a strong nation. How does his drawing help to send this message?

Draw a picture of a crowd. You might draw a party or people watching a ball game. Where else do you see crowds of people? Could you draw crowds of animals, trees and other kinds of things? Could you make your drawing like an editorial cartoon that sends a message to people?

 Student artwork.

Creating a Feeling of Action
Showing People in Motion

Edgar Degas, *Ballet Scene,* ca.1907. Pastel on cardboard, 30 1/4 x 43 3/4" (79 x 111 cm). National Gallery of Art, Washington, DC (Chester Dale Collection).

What games, sports and action-packed activities do you like? Do you like to skate, swim or dance?

These artworks show people, or figures, in action. The feeling of action comes from the bends in the body. Do you see the **angles** in the arms, legs, wrists and ankles? How else have the artists shown action and movement?

In each artwork, the figures fill most of the space. This kind of design makes you feel close to the action. The largest figures are nearly as tall as the height of the picture. The smaller figures are in the background. What else helps you see action in near and far spaces?

When you overlap shapes, you create **perspective**. You help people see which figures are in front of each other. Look at the perspective in picture A. The large figure on the right overlaps the other dancers near her. Where do you see overlapping shapes in picture B?

Look again at the background spaces in each artwork. Where do you see people that look close to the bottom of the picture? Why does this position make these figures look near to you?

Create an artwork with figures in action. Choose an activity you like and know about. Sketch some figures with angles, or bends, that show motion.

Plan your artwork so that it has perspective. How can you show figures that are near and farther away?

29

Observing Details
Exploring Nature Upclose

Have you ever studied the shapes, colors and patterns in insects? Have you ever tried to show their details in a realistic artwork?

Insects are shown in the artworks of many lands. In many cultures, insects are also **symbols** for ideas. Bees, for example, are often symbols for good things that come from hard work.

In many parts of Asia, people admire the beauty of insects. Insects are also symbols for this idea: Very small things are important in nature and in our lives. Can you think of other ways that insects could be symbols for ideas?

An artist in Japan created the scroll painting in picture A. A **scroll** painting is made on cloth. As you unroll the scroll, you see many beautiful sections. The scroll can also be hung on a wall so you can see all of it.

This painting is filled with many insects. They are shown in a natural environment near a stream. You discover the insects one-by-one. The delicate shapes of the insects and plants create a lace-like design. What are some other important elements in this painting?

 Maekawa Bunrei, *Flowers and Insects,* 1909. The British Library, London, and The Bridgeman Art Library, London (Private collection).

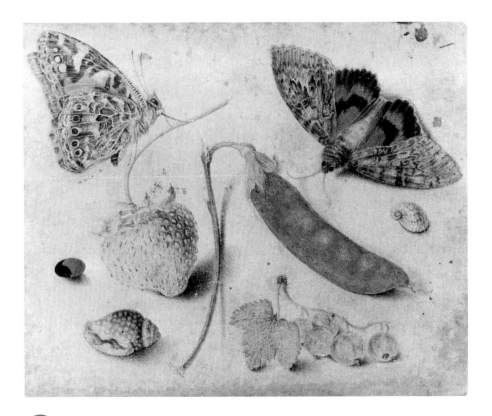

Albrecht Dürer, *Stag Beetle,*
1505. Watercolor and gouache,
5 9/16 x 4 1/2" (14 x 11 cm).
Collection of the J. Paul Getty
Museum, Malibu, California.

Maria Sibylla Merian, *Studies from Nature: butterfly,
moth, strawberry, pea pod, white currants, shells,* ca.
1700. Watercolor on vellum, 4 5/16 x 3 1/2" (11 x 9 cm).
The Metropolitan Museum of Art (Fletcher Fund, 1939).

The paintings in pictures B and C were made by artists who lived in Europe over 300 years ago.

The artist who painted *Studies from Nature* became well-known as a scientist. She studied butterflies, moths and other insects in Europe and South America. Many of her paintings show the life cycle of an insect and the food that it eats. Her paintings became illustrations for three books.

The painting *Stag Beetle* is one of many **subjects** that this artist explored. His beetle seems to be moving across the paper. He has shown a closeup view of one insect and its shadow.

Imagine you have discovered a new species of insect. No one has seen it before. Create a **close-up** illustration that looks realistic. You might work with classmates to create a scroll painting with many new kinds of insects.

30

Exploring Media
Stitching a Picture

Did you know that a needle and thread can be used to create artwork? An artwork created by sewing, or stitching, is **stitchery**.

Many different yarns and threads can be used for stitchery. The stitches can be long or short. They can be close together or make outlines.

Look at picture A. What kind of stitch would be best to outline a shape? Which stitch could you use to fill in a shape? How might you use a cross-stitch? What other stitches can you invent?

B *The Pheasant in the Tree,* 1830. Embroidered silk thread on paper, 12 1/16 x 15 3/8" (39 x 31 cm). The St. Louis Art Museum (Museum Purchase).

Tie a knot near the end.

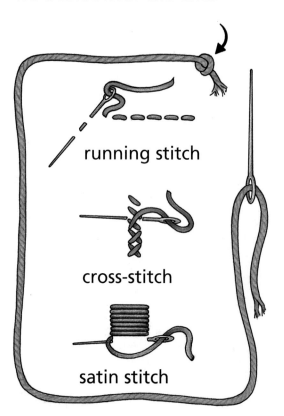

running stitch

cross-stitch

satin stitch

A

The **embroidery**, or stitchery, in picture B was created about 150 years ago. This American artist created the stitches in paper with silk thread.

Birds were a popular subject for stitching and other artwork in the 1830s. Some of this new interest came from the pictures of birds in a book by John J. Audubon.

Kantha, detail from ceremonial quilt, Indian, East Bengal,19th century. Embroidery, two layers of white cotton sari fabric, 72 1/2 x 46 1/4" (194 x 118 cm). The Cleveland Museum of Art (Gift of the Textile Arts Club).

Student artwork.

Study the stitching in the quilt from India. A **quilt** is a hand-made blanket with several layers of cloth. This quilt shows an elephant. In India, elephants are symbols of good luck.

Where do you see zigzag stitches? Where do you see outlines made with thread? What other stitches can you see? Can you figure out how they were created?

You can create a stitched artwork. You might want to do some practice stitches on a scrap of cloth. You might choose an animal or another idea for your work. Make sketches. Plan the main shapes and lines. Draw these lightly on your cloth.

Stitching should be done slowly and carefully. It takes time to make well-crafted work. After you complete the stitching, you might add some other materials, such as buttons, beads or pieces of ribbon.

 Linda Stevens, *Haiku #4,* 1984. Courtesy of the artist.

In this unit, you have learned about some styles of art. A style of art comes from the way an artist designs, or plans, every part of the artwork. The name of an art style helps you remember how artworks are alike and different.

You have also explored different subjects and themes for art. Use what you have learned to see and think about the artworks in this lesson.

These artworks have one main **theme**. All of them show living things in or near water. Can you also see differences in the style of these artworks?

Look at the painting in picture A. It is done in a **realistic** style. The textures, colors and details remind you of a real scene. A realistic painting can look as real as a photograph. Do you think this painting is as realistic as a photograph? Why or why not?

Now look at the drawing in picture B. Does it look as realistic as the painting of water lilies? Would it be better to say the drawing of the shell is somewhat abstract? **Abstract** means the artist leaves out some details. Do you think the painting combines realistic and abstract styles? Why or why not?

 Georgia O'Keeffe, *Pink Shell with Seaweed,* 1938. Pastel, 22 x 28" (56 x 71 cm). San Diego Museum of Art (Gift of Mrs. Norton Walbridge).

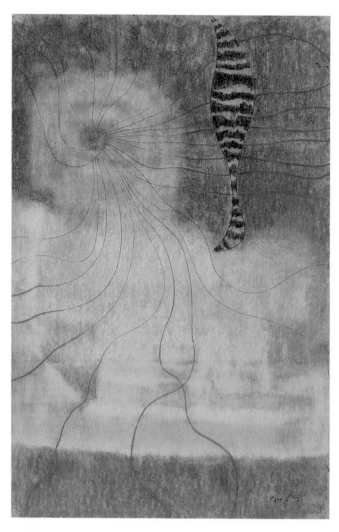

 William Baziotes, *Sea Forms,* 1951. Pastel on paper on masonite, 38 1/8 x 25 1/8" (97 x 64 cm). Collection of Whitney Museum of American Art, New York. Photograph: Gamma One Conversions, New York.

Now look at the drawing in picture C. Lines and shapes seem to float and drift in a colorful sea. Can you find any realistic elements? The drawing shows an imaginary scene. You could call this style **fantasy art** or abstract-fantasy. What other style names might be used for this artwork?

The artworks in this lesson are different in size and shape. They are different in design and materials. Which artworks are most alike? Why?

With your classmates and teachers, choose a theme for an art project. Discuss the subjects that go with your theme. Choose one of the subjects and create an artwork in your own style.

After you have created your work, invent a style name for it. The style name can combine words like realistic, abstract or fantasy. Can you invent other names for your style?

Art to See and Use
Art in Your Environment

B Wayne Ngan. National Museums of Canada, Ottawa.
Photograph: Rolf Bettner.

Do you know people who have jobs, or **careers**, in art?

Teaching art is a good career if you like to help people learn new things. Most cities have many places where people can learn about art. One of these places is an art museum.

The man in picture A is a docent in a museum. A **docent** is a guide and teacher for people who visit the museum. Docents learn about the history of artworks. They learn about the artists who created the artworks too. What are some other careers for people who like to study and teach art history?

Wayne Ngan, in picture B, is a **craftsworker** in ceramics. He makes pottery from clay. He lives on a Canadian island. He says that the beauty of nature gives him ideas for pottery. He has also learned about ceramics by studying ancient pottery from his homeland in China.

D Photograph: Ann Hawthorne for The Penland School.

C Michelle V. Agins. Photograph: Bob Black.

Many artists have careers that help people in a community. Michelle V. Agins, in picture C, was a **photographer** for the mayor's office in Chicago, Illinois. Her photographs show important events in the city.

Have you ever used a camera? Can you think of other art careers in business or government?

Sometimes artists have skills they can use in more than one job. The person in picture D is welding a sculpture from metal. She is using a special helmet, gloves and suit. This **safety equipment** protects her from the hot sparks. She can also find other jobs as a welder of metal.

What are some other skills that can be used for art? What careers do you like to think about? How does art fit into them? In this unit you will learn more about art that people in your community create, see and use.

31

Industrial Design
Designing a Better Product

B *Ventaglio sink.* Designer: Bruno Gecchelin. Courtesy of Thelma Guzzini.

A *Newspaper vending box.* Rotationally molded polyethylene. Design: Brooks Stevens Design Associates. Courtesy of Fortec, Inc. Photograph: John Sinchok.

Are you an inventor? Do you like to create designs for cars, toys or other things that could be made in a factory? Many people do this kind of work. Engineers plan many parts of factory-made products.

Artists called **industrial designers** work with engineers. Industrial designers plan the way a product looks. They plan the surfaces people touch and the forms people hold or move, like handles or latches.

Industrial designers think about the colors, shapes and textures that a product might have. They create sketches of these ideas before the product is manufactured.

Look at the examples of factory-made objects in this lesson. What parts help you know an industrial designer planned them?

Scout Discoverer Wheelchair, 1981. Designer: Douglas Ball. Courtesy of Douglas Ball Inc., Quebec, Canada.

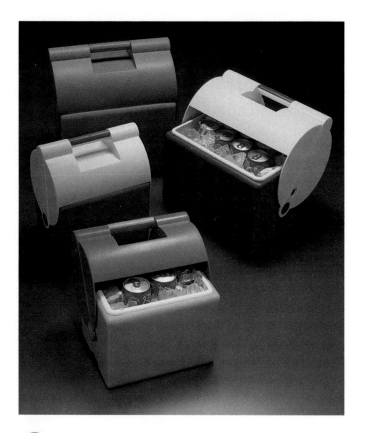

 Playmate II Coolers. Manufactured by Igloo Product Corp. for Crown Corning. Designers: James J. Costello, William Prindle.

Industrial designers like to solve problems. They often try to improve the design of a product that many people will use.

The wheelchair design in picture D is one example of problem-solving. A Canadian designer wanted to plan a wheelchair for children. He thought a good design should be easy and fun to use. He knew the design must be safe and help a person feel secure.

This chair has a battery and a motor. The steering control is near the lap. Four wheels move the chair in any direction. Most children can learn to use the chair quickly. What other parts have been carefully planned? Can you think of ways it could be improved?

Choose a product that you use very often. Think about ways to improve the design. Make sketches of your new design.

32

Graphic Design
Designing a Package

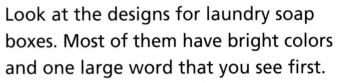

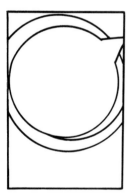

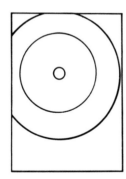

A

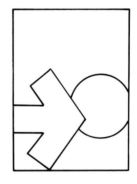

B

C

Look at the designs for laundry soap boxes. Most of them have bright colors and one large word that you see first.

Artists called **graphic designers** created these designs. They planned the lettering you see. They designed the lines, the colors and all the shapes on the package.

Find the package with a large arrow and circle in pictures A and B. Do you think the large shapes and bold letters go with the name of the soap?

Look at the diagrams in picture C. Find the packages with similar lines and shapes. Why do you think so many packages have swirling curves or circles?

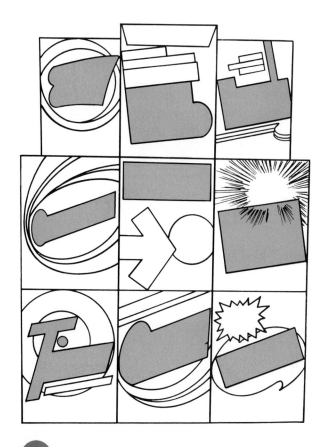

D

Look at picture D. The shaded parts are similar to the large letters on each soap box.

Most of the brand names on the soap packages are slanted upward. The diagonal lines suggest a feeling of action or motion.

What other things do you notice in these designs for soap boxes? Why are soap names and box designs so carefully planned?

The designs on the boxes in picture E have been changed about five times in the last 80 years. Why do you think the designs were changed?

Imagine you are a graphic designer for a cereal company. Draw a design for the front of a new cereal box.

E

Lettering
Inventing New Alphabets

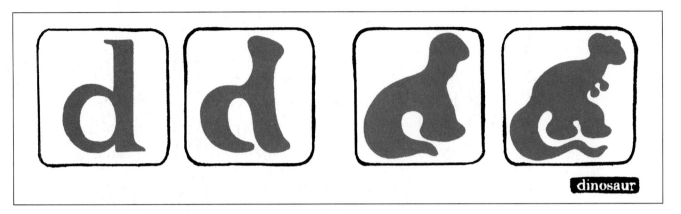

dinosaur

A Original art for *The Alphabet Book,* 1952. Designer: Dorothy Schmiderer.

Graphic designers plan the **lettering** in many things you see. Some artists like to be inventive with letters of the alphabet. If you are **inventive**, you have ideas no one else has thought about.

Look at picture A. Do you see how the artist has changed the letter "d" into a picture? This design is from an alphabet book. How do you think the designer changed other letters in the book? How could you change a letter into a picture?

What letter has been changed in the stamp design in picture B? Can you still read the main word in the stamp? Why?

B Designer: Bradbury Thompson, 1984.

Designer: Jeanine Colini.

Some graphic designers invent new kinds of alphabets. Picture C shows four letters from an alphabet. The letters have been changed to look like animals. Why do you think designers like to invent new alphabets?

Students created the letters in picture D. They drew their initials. Then they changed each letter to show something else. They made each shape into a picture.

See if you can invent some picture letters for your name, or initials, or a short word you like. Let the shapes of the letters give you ideas for the pictures you invent.

D Student artwork.

United States

Norway

Canada

Cuba

Malaysia

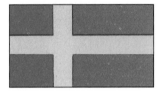
Sweden

Mexico

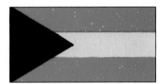
Bahamas

Imagine you could see every flag of every nation. You would be looking at more than 160 flags. You can see many flags at the Olympic Games and the United Nations building in New York City. You can find pictures of flags in books.

The flag of each nation has many visual symbols. A **visual symbol** is made of lines, colors and shapes that stand for something else.

People who live in a nation learn the meaning of visual symbols in their flag. In the United States' flag, the thirteen stripes stand for the thirteen colonies that helped set up the laws for this nation. Find the flag of Malaysia on this page. The fourteen stripes stand for the separate states in that nation.

Most flags have pure, bright colors like you see in the color wheel. Many nations also use black or white as colors. The colors in most flags are symbols.

In many nations, red and black are symbols of strength, endurance and sacrifice. Green is often a symbol for growth, or thanksgiving for nature. How could you find out the meaning of colors in a nation's flag?

United Kingdom

Japan

Jamaica

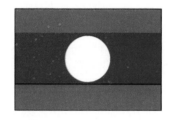
Laos

Create a flag design for yourself. Study the examples in pictures B and C. Use shapes and colors that have special meaning to you. What other symbols have special meaning to you?

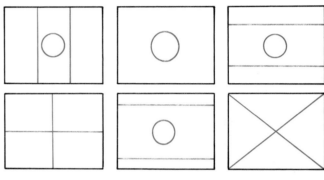

B

Most flags are designed in the shape of a rectangle. The colors, shapes and spaces are usually very simple so the whole design is easy to see.

Over fifty countries have flags with three **horizontal** stripes or three **vertical** stripes. Sometimes the center band has a symbol. Look at picture A. The flags of Canada, Mexico and Laos have this plan.

Look at the other flag designs. Some flags have similar spaces and shapes. They have special symbols and colors to make each one unique. **Unique** means unlike any others.

The left and right sides of these flag designs are alike. In some designs, the top and bottom are alike. This kind of balance is called **symmetry**.

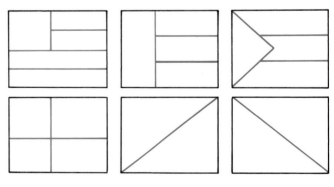

C

The spaces in these flags are balanced, but they are not alike on each side. This kind of balance is called **asymmetry**.

35

Cartoons and Caricatures
Drawing Caricatures

 Toba Sojo, *Frolic Animals (Choju-Giga)* (detail),12th century. Ink on paper, 11 7/8" (30 cm) high. Collection of Kozan-ji Temple, Kyoto, Japan.

Have you ever seen frogs and a rabbit chasing a monkey with a hat? If you are thinking like a scientist, your answer would be "no." If you are thinking like an artist, your answer might be "yes."

Many people enjoy stories and cartoons that show animals acting like people. Experts do not know when or where the first cartoon-like pictures of animals were made, but they have been found in many lands.

About 800 years ago in Japan, an artist created a long scroll painting with animals acting like people. A detail from this scroll is shown in picture A. How can you tell that this drawing is meant to be humorous, like a **cartoon**?

The animals in picture A are an example of caricature. In a **caricature**, you see a likeness of something, but parts are changed. The changes help to express the personality or character of something. The frogs, rabbit and monkey have human-like features. What parts of the animals have been changed to make them more like people?

Gary Baseman, Illustration for *Boston Globe Magazine,* ca. 1988. Courtesy of the artist.

In picture B, you see a present-day caricature of animals. This cartoon was created for a newspaper story about housekeeping. Why do you think the newspaper editor wanted a cartoon for this story? What parts of the dogs have been changed to create caricatures?

Create some caricatures of animals. Choose animals you like to draw. Show the animal doing something that only people can really do. For example, you might draw a dog riding a bike or driving a car. You might draw a fish eating an ice cream cone.

After you have made some sketches, change other parts to make the animal a caricature. For example, you might draw eyes shaped like circles, diamonds or squares. The center parts of the eyes might look up, down or to one side. Can you think of other ways to create a caricature?

36 Humorous Illustrations
Creating Picture Puzzles

 A Photograph of Norman Rockwell. Courtesy of Fritz Henning.

 B **Norman Rockwell,** *Dugout* (detail). Reprinted from *The Saturday Evening Post* ©1943. Reprinted by Permission of the Norman Rockwell Family Trust.

Norman Rockwell was one of America's most famous illustrators. An **illustrator** is an artist who creates pictures that explain something or tell a story.

Picture A shows Norman Rockwell at work in his studio. He is creating a sketch for a magazine cover. A detail of the finished artwork is shown in picture B. What idea does the illustration show? How did the artist help you know the feelings of the players?

Norman Rockwell created his illustrations by making many sketches of the whole design, or **composition**. The sketches helped him decide how to pose the people. The sketches helped him plan the background and details.

After he sketched a composition, he asked people to come to his studio to pose. He liked to observe and draw portraits of people. If the people could not spend time posing, he would photograph them. How do you think he studied other details, such as the leather glove?

Norman Rockwell, *April Fool*. Reprinted from The *Saturday Evening Post* ©1943. Reprinted by Permission of the Norman Rockwell Family Trust.

Picture C shows one of Norman Rockwell's most inventive illustrations. It is a visual puzzle with over 100 strange details. How many can you find? Why might people enjoy finding the odd parts?

William Henry Fox Talbot, *Botanical Specimen,* 1839. Photogenic drawing. Printroom, University of Leiden, The Netherlands.

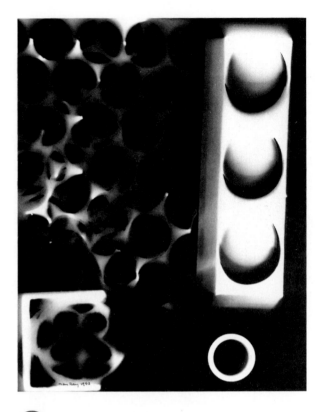

Man Ray, *Untitled,* 1943. Rayogram, 14 3/16 x 11" (36 x 28 cm). Denver Art Museum, Colorado (Gift of Mr. and Mrs. Walter Maitland).

Picture A shows one of the earliest kinds of **photographs**, a shadowgram. The shadowgram was made in 1839 by William Henry Fox Talbot, an inventor and scientist from England. His delicate records of leaves astonished people of his time. His pictures seemed to be more real than any image created with paint, crayon or other media.

Shadowgrams are now called photograms. A **photogram** is a record of shadows made on a special paper. The paper changes when light strikes its surface.

If you place objects on the paper and then expose the design to light, you have a record of the shadows and silhouettes of the objects.

The process of making photograms is fascinating. The objects you place on the paper can leave unusual shadows. Look at picture B. What objects might have created the design in Man Ray's photogram?

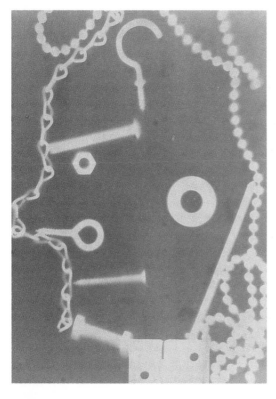

 C   Student artwork.

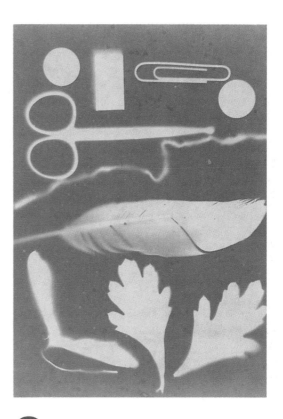

D   Student artwork.

You can create images similar to photograms. Collect objects that are nearly flat, such as leaves, twigs, vines and small feathers. Other objects might be scraps of paper, buttons, coins, paper clips, yarn or lace. Put a piece of paper or a piece of stiff cardboard on a tray.

Arrange the objects on top of the paper. Each object will stop sunlight from reaching the paper. When the photogram is finished, the paper will be a record of shadows or silhouettes of each object.

Plan your work around one or more design principles. Some objects may suggest a theme such as a face, a robot or a strange landscape. Students created the photograms in pictures C and D. Can you see how the objects suggested design ideas? They used paper known as blueprint or sunprint paper.

Your teacher will give you special instructions on how to finish your photogram. The photogram will be made by exposing your design to bright light.

 The Evolution of Mickey Mouse, 1988. ©The Walt Disney Company.

Not too long ago, Mickey Mouse had his 60th birthday. Walt Disney invented this well-known cartoon character in 1928.

Picture A shows how this character has been redesigned over sixty years. On the left, you see the first version of the mouse. On the right, you see more recent versions. What differences do you see in the eyes and other features?

Cartoon characters can be people or animals. Why do you think cartoons with animals acting like people are so popular?

The cartoons in films and television are made from thousands of pictures. Each picture is just a little different from the others. When the pictures are shown very quickly, you see the **illusion** of movement. What changes help to suggest movement in pictures B, C and D?

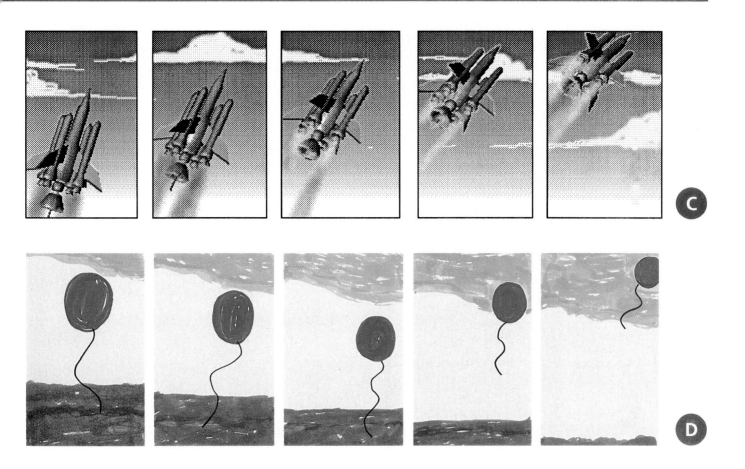

C

D

The art of creating cartoons for films and television is called animation. An **animator** is an artist who helps draw the cartoons. An animated show is often planned by making flip books.

To make a flip book, think of something that moves and how it moves.

Put five index cards down. On the first card, draw the beginning of the motion. On the last card, draw the end of the motion. Use the center card to draw the middle of the action. Now finish the other two cards. These cards will show small changes.

Stack your cards in order. Hold them tightly in one hand. With the thumb of your other hand, flip the cards from the top to the bottom. You can also restack the cards and flip them from the bottom to the top.

Ludwig Mies van der Rohe, *Lake Shore Drive Apartment Houses,* Chicago, 1950–1952. Photograph: George Barford.

Look for forms like these in buildings. These forms have curved edges.

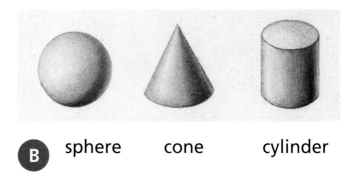

B   sphere   cone   cylinder

These forms have straight edges.

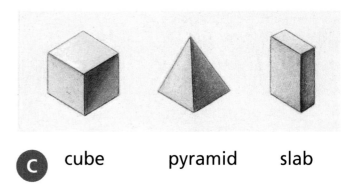

C   cube   pyramid   slab

Architects are artists who design buildings. They plan the forms you see in a building. The forms are designed to be walls, roofs and other parts of the building.

Many architects combine **forms** like cones, cylinders and cubes in one building. Sometimes a whole building has one main form, like a pyramid. Picture A shows two buildings with slab-like forms. Are there similar buildings in your town?

 Susana Torre, *Fire Station Five,* Columbus, Indiana. Photograph: Timothy Hursley, The Arkansas Office.

Architect Susana Torre designed this fire station. Do you see two cylinders in her design? The center **tower** has a circular staircase inside. The other tower is used to dry hoses. What other forms do you see? How are they used?

 Architect's model, 1985. Schoeler & Heaton Architects, Inc., Ontario, Canada.

Architects make models to show the design of a building. What forms do you see in this model? What details do you see? Details are small parts, such as windows and doors.

Make a model of a building. Use small boxes, paper cups and other forms. You can make some forms from paper. Use glue and tape to join the forms. How can you add details?

Mark a paper. Fold it.

Make two. Paste. Add a roof.

Make other forms.

pyramid   cone

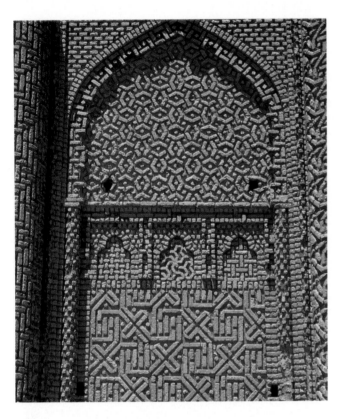

 A *Kharraccum Tomb Tower*, Iran, 11th century. Brickwork. Robert Harding Picture Library, London, England.

B *Computer Logics Building.* Courtesy of Stark, Hicks, Spragge Architects, Ontario, Canada.

Have you ever noticed the **textures** and **patterns** in buildings? Concrete, wood, bricks and other **materials** can be put together in many patterns.

The building in picture A has fancy brickwork, like a relief sculpture. Parts of the design are raised up from a flat background. This **mosque** was built over 900 years ago by Islamic artists in Iran.

In many buildings today, patterns are created by smooth materials such as glass, steel and plastic. An architect

in Canada designed the building in picture B. The patterns are created by squares and rectangles of metal. Which shapes are made from glass? Why are the glass shapes in rows?

Many buildings have textures and patterns from different materials. The house in picture C is in The Netherlands. The house has smooth bricks on the exterior, or outside. Can you find other textures and patterns?

 C

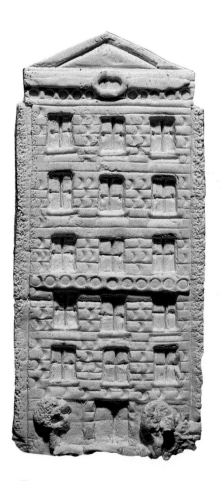

 D   Student artwork.

Sketch some textures and patterns of wood, brick and other building materials. Think about the reasons architects choose these materials.

You can explore textures and patterns for buildings in other ways. You might create a relief sculpture. Make a flat slab of clay about as thick as your thumb. Practice making patterns and textures by pressing objects into clay. After you experiment, make your relief sculpture. A student made the relief sculpture in picture D.

E

Flying-Cloud Pavilion (Hiunkaku), Kyoto, Japan, 1594. Courtesy of Nishi-Honganji.

A Japanese Shogun, or ruler, built this palace about 400 years ago. He planned the pond and garden, too. Designing parks and gardens is an ancient form of art. In China and Japan, many people plan beautiful gardens. The gardens are places to see and think about natural beauty.

This garden has an informal or **asymmetrical** design. The low round bushes make an irregular pattern around the pond and bridge. The plants are not the same in height. Some are closer together than others. What other things make this an asymmetrical design for a garden?

Michael Graves, *San Juan Capistrano Regional Library,* San Juan Capistrano, California.
Photograph ©1986 by Bruce Iverson.

This library in California has a courtyard with a small park. A **courtyard** is an outdoor space with walls around it. This park has formal, or **symmetrical**, balance. In this kind of balance, the left and the right sides look alike. The trees are alike. They are evenly spaced. What other parts make it a symmetrical design?

Today, artists who design gardens, parks and other outdoor spaces are called **landscape architects**. Learn about parks and gardens in your community. Who plans them? Why do people want them?

Think about a garden or park you would like. Then draw or create a collage of your design.

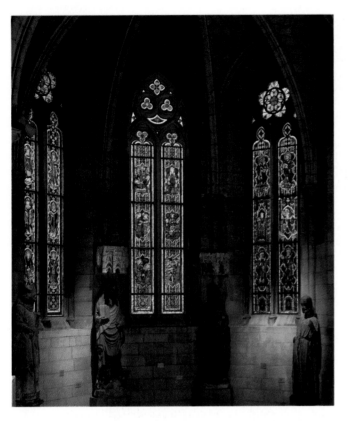

A

Stained glass windows from St. Leonard, Lavanthal, Austria, ca. 1340. The Metropolitan Museum of Art, New York (The Cloisters Collection).

B

Courtesy of Hirschberg Design Group, Toronto, Canada—J.J. Muggs.

For hundreds of years, architects and artists have been fascinated with the way light can create beauty inside of buildings.

Long ago in Europe, people built great churches. One of these is shown in picture A. The windows are made of **stained glass**. The pieces of colored glass fit together like parts of a puzzle. Natural light from the sun comes through the glass. The gleaming colors from the windows are an inspiration to people who go to the church.

Today, many buildings have colored electric lights. You see these bright lights in stores and many signs at night. In large shopping centers, you may see bright electric lights during the daytime. What kind of **lighting** do you see in picture B?

Artists explore light and color in other ways. Some create spaces with lighted sculptures, such as the environment in picture C. Others design lighted signs and displays for people to see at night.

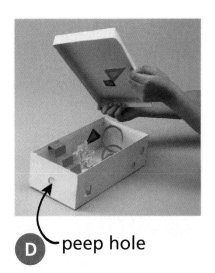

 McCrystle Wood, *Installation,* 1988. Light and mixed media, 20 x 8 x 12' (6 x 2.4 x 3.6 m). Courtesy of the artist.

D ⤴ peep hole

Fold paper in half. Fold it again. Make a few holes. Cover the holes with colored cellophane or tissue paper. Paste the tube. Trace and cut two triangles for the ends of the tube.

You can do some experiments with colored lighting. Find a shoebox with a lid (see picture D) or make a tube (see picture E). Make holes in the container like tiny windows. The holes will let light inside the container.

Make a small sculpture from white paper or aluminum foil to put inside your container. Add other forms. What happens when you look through the peep hole?

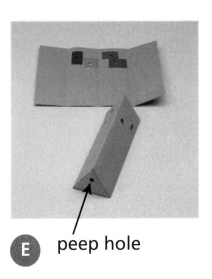

E peep hole

43 Stained Glass Windows
Seeing Color and Light

A **Unknown, *Rose Window,*** Cathedral of Notre Dame, 13th century. Stained glass. Photograph: Giraudon/Art Resource, New York.

B **John Forbes and Jeanne Rosen, *Residential dome skylight.*** Stained glass. Courtesy of Bonny Doon Art Glass, Santa Cruz, California.

The stained glass window in picture A is a detail of a larger window. This window was created for a church in Europe over 700 years ago. Windows such as these brought glowing light into the dark interior of churches. Many of the small circles in this window show events and people from the Bible.

The window in picture B was recently created for a home. It has shapes that come from natural forms such as leaves. Do you see other shapes from nature?

Both of the windows have radial balance. In **radial balance**, shapes and lines go out from a center. You see radial designs in many flowers and wheels. Where else have you seen radial balance?

Sometimes stained glass is **transparent**, like the color in cellophane or sunglasses. Sometimes the colors are translucent. **Translucent** means a color or surface glows from light, but you can't see details through it.

You can explore translucent color by using tissue paper and diluted white glue. You can also learn to cut radial designs from paper. You can display your work in a window to see the translucent colors.

How will your artwork be similar to stained glass? Why will it be very different?

1. Cut a square. Fold the square twice. Trim the corners to make a circle. Cut shapes in the folded edges. Unfold.

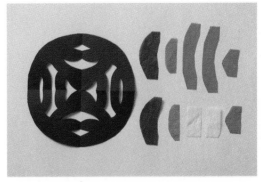

2. Cut colored tissue paper. This paper will cover the holes in the circle. Choose colors to create a balanced design.

3. Trace the circle on wax paper. Cut the wax paper. Paste the two circles together. With the wax paper facing you, glue the tissue paper down. Let the work dry before you display it.

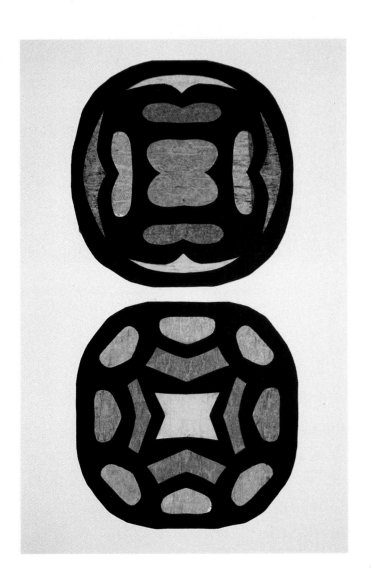

C

101

44 Landmarks
Symbols in Spaces

 Simon Rodia, *Watts Towers,* Los Angeles, California, 1921–1954. Courtesy of Duane Preble.

 Eero Saarinen, *Gateway Arch,* St. Louis, Missouri, 1959–64. Courtesy of St. Louis Convention and Visitors Bureau.

Simon Rodia built the towers in picture A from steel and cement. He covered them with pieces of tile and other colorful things he found. The tallest tower is 99 1/2 feet (30.3 m). The towers are a landmark in the Watts section of Los Angeles, California.

A **landmark** is a place in a neighborhood or town that almost every person knows about. The graceful arch in picture B is in St. Louis, Missouri. It is 62 stories high. A famous architect designed this landmark.

Are there historical landmarks where you live? Historical landmarks are old buildings or places that help people remember the past.

The church in picture C is in Charleston, South Carolina. It is more than 230 years old. Many people have helped to take care of it for many years. Towns with old, well-cared-for landmarks help people remember the past.

A landmark does not have to be a famous or unusual building. It is a place or building people want to see, visit or remember.

The park in picture D is a landmark for children who live near it. Can you explain why?

Choose a landmark to draw. Keep it a secret. When everyone has finished drawing, ask if anyone else drew the same landmark.

C *St. Michael's Church,* 1752–61. Charleston, South Carolina.

D *Elm Park,* Worcester, Massachusetts. Photograph: Roy Bourgeault.

Historical Preservation
Preserving Special Buildings

 Taj Mahal, Agra, India, 1632–53.
Courtesy of Comstock, Inc./Bonnie Kamin.

Around the world, people create buildings for special reasons. They build homes to live in. They create places for worship. Sometimes they construct buildings to honor the memory of people.

The buildings you see here were constructed long ago in different countries. Each one has a special purpose. Each one is cared for as if it were a great treasure. Some people call these buildings masterpieces of architecture. A **masterpiece** is an artwork that many people have admired for a long time.

The Taj Mahal in picture A is in India. It honors the memory of a woman. It is a memorial building. The building is covered with sparkling pieces of white and colored stone. Some parts have delicate carving and colorful borders.

B *Golden Pavilion*, Kyoto, Japan, 1398.

C *St. Basil's Cathedral,* Moscow, 1554–1560.
Photograph: S. Vidler, Superstock, Inc.

The building in picture B is in Japan. It was constructed about 600 years ago. It was built as a study space for a military ruler. It has a library and a collection of artworks. It has **balconies** so that people can look out on the beautiful pond and trees. The curved roofs help to drain the snow and rain away from the building.

The church in picture C is in Russia. The building has many fancy patterns of brick and stone. Some of the surfaces are painted with many colors.

Most communities have buildings that are very special. Think about a building in your community that is a special treasure to you. It should be a building you would like everyone to admire and take care of for a long time. Draw a picture of it.

A **Helen Escobedo, *The Great Cone,*** 1987, Jerusalem, Israel. Steel, 26' 3" x 23' (8 x 7 m). Courtesy of the artist.

B Helen Escobedo. Courtesy of
Galeria Sloane Racotta, Mexico.

In this unit, you have learned about many careers in
art. Some people have more than one job or career
in art. Mexican artist Helen Escobedo designed the
"see-through" sculptures in pictures A and C. She
knows that her **outdoor sculpture** will look
different with changes in the time of day and
weather. She plans her work so these changes in
light, color and shadow are part of the design.

Each sculpture is planned for one **site**, or location.
The artist wants her sculpture to help people see
and think about the location in a new way.

C   **Helen Escobedo,** *Coatl (snake),* 1982. Steel I-beams, 19' 6" x 48' 9" (6 x 15 m). National University of Mexico.

Helen Escobedo has created sculptures in Mexico, Israel, the United States and Europe. She speaks five languages. She is often called an "international artist." Do you know what this phrase means?

This remarkable artist also writes about art. She designed her own home. She has also been the director of the Museum of Modern Art in Mexico City.

Choose an artist you admire. Do some research to learn more about the artist. You might interview an artist you know. You could do library research to learn about an artist from the past.

After you have done your research, share what you have learned with the class. Your report could be written or it could be a short talk. You might work with other students to create a short play about an artist's life and work.

 A ***Decorated Easter Eggs,*** 20th century, Czechoslovakia. Eggs, dye, 1 7/8 x 2 3/4 x 1 7/8" (5 x 7 x 5 cm). National Museum of American History, Smithsonian Institution, Washington, DC.

The artwork in this lesson is called traditional art. **Traditional art** is often made or used in the same way year after year. The art helps people remember ideas, stories and times that are important to them.

In Eastern Europe, people have a tradition of decorating eggs during the spring. The eggs are given as gifts near Easter, a Christian holiday. The designs are symbols for the sun, living things and nature's beauty in spring.

B ***Battledore,*** ca. 1875–1946, Japan. Wood, silk, brocade, paper, watercolor, 24 x 9 x 2" (61 x 23 x 5 cm). National Museum of Natural History, Smithsonian Institution, Washington, DC.

People in many countries create art for gifts, decorations and special holidays. For New Year's Day in Japan, children often receive or give paddle-shaped gifts like the one in picture B.

C ***Shadow Puppet,*** Kelantan Province, Malaysia, 19th century. National Museum of Natural History, Smithsonian Institution, Washington, DC.

In Indonesia and Malaysia, people create leather puppets (see picture C). They use the puppets to tell their favorite stories and celebrate special events, such as birthdays.

The puppets are held so that they cast a shadow on a white sheet. Long sticks are used to move parts of the shadow puppets.

The use of fireworks for celebrations began in China. Today, people in many lands celebrate national holidays with displays of fireworks.

In this unit you will learn about some traditional kinds of art and how present-day artists explore them.

Sake Pourer, Arita ware, Imari style, 17th century. Porcelain underglaze; blue overglaze; enamels and gold. The Seattle Art Museum, Washington (Purchased with funds from the Sue M. Naef Estate, in memory of her husband, Aubrey A. Naef).

Nampeyo Pottery, ca. 1900. Wounded Knee Gallery. Photograph: Dick Friske.

Portrait Stirrup Vessel, Chimbote Valley, 300–500 A.D. Ceramic, slip and paint, 11 1/2 " (29 cm) high. Denver Art Museum, Colorado (Gift of Mr. and Mrs. Frederick R. Mayer).

Pottery is a container created by hand from ceramic clay. **Ceramic clay** is soft moist earth. After the clay is shaped, the work is allowed to dry. Then it is baked in a special oven called a **kiln** (say kill). This step is known as **firing** the clay because the kiln gets as hot as a fire.

A glassy surface on pottery is glaze. A **glaze** is a mixture of water and minerals. When a pot is fired in a kiln, the minerals melt. Glaze adds color to the clay and makes it **waterproof**.

Clay for pottery is often found near rivers. This is one reason why pottery is made in many lands. Pottery is also one of the oldest art forms.

The forms and decorations on pottery can be beautiful and have special meaning. Look at the pottery in this lesson. Why do you think the containers have different forms? Why do they have decorations?

Chinese Bowl, Northern Sung dynasty, 11th–12th century A.D. Yaozhou ware, stoneware with translucent grayish-green glaze, 8" (20 cm) diameter. The Art Institute of Chicago (Bequest of Russell Tyson, 1964). Photograph ©1991, The Art Institute of Chicago. All Rights Reserved.

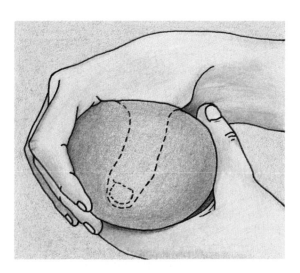

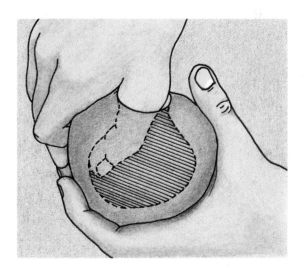

You can learn to create pottery. The pinch method is one of the oldest ways to create a pot. Study the steps in picture E.

1. Press your thumb into the center of a ball of clay. Turn the ball, pressing the clay between your thumb and fingers.

2. Keep turning the ball, pressing the clay from the bottom toward the top.

3. Place three fingers on the top edge as you turn the pot. Make a smooth, strong edge.

Finish the design. You might add a handle or make a lid for your pot. You can create textures or patterns on the surface. What other ideas do you have?

 Unknown, *Mosaic Mirror,* Peru, 8th–13th century. Turquoise, pyrites and shell, 9 7/16 x 4 3/4 x 3/4" (24 x 12 x 2 cm). Dumbarton Oaks Research Library and Collections, Washington, DC.

B ***Pair of Ear Ornaments,*** Peru, Mochica, ca. 200–500 A.D. Gold with semi-precious stones, 4" (10 cm).

Look at the mirror and the earrings in pictures A and B. These artworks were created long ago by artists from Peru in South America. They are examples of pre-Columbian art. **Pre-Columbian** refers to art created before Christopher Columbus and other Europeans came to the Americas.

Pre-Columbian art was created in South America, Central America and North America. This ancient art helps us know about the history of the first people in the Americas.

The mirror and the earrings are mosaic artworks. A **mosaic** is made of small pieces of colored stone, shells or other materials. The pieces are placed next to each other, like parts of a

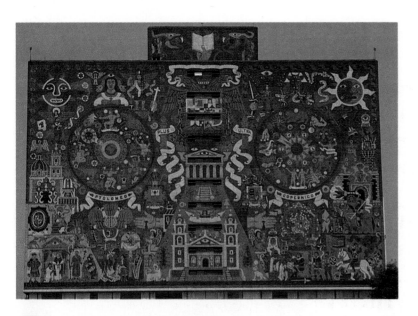

 Juan O'Gorman, *The University Library, Mexico City,* 1950–52. Photograph ©Ulrike Welsch.

 D

puzzle. They can be put into plaster, or glued on a stiff surface.

Ideas from pre-Columbian art have inspired many present-day artists in Mexico. You can see this influence in picture C. The design in this mural tells about the history of Mexico. The mural has many visual symbols from pre-Columbian and later times in Mexico. Why do you think the artist used mosaic for the mural?

You can create a mosaic collage. Plan a simple design. Think of a visual symbol that tells about your own history. What special things are part of your past? What other ideas might express your history?

Sketch your ideas. Plan your color scheme with crayons. What other design elements should you think about?

Cut or tear strips of colored paper. Cut or tear across the strip to make squares and other small shapes. Glue the pieces for the main lines and shapes first. Place them side by side. Then fill the rest of the space.

Papier-Mâché Sculpture
Creating a Toy

 Unknown, *Tiger of Shinno Shrine (Shinno-No-Tora) and Red Cow,* 1979. Painted papier-mâché with bobbing head, 5 x 7 " (13 x 18 cm). Collection of Mingei International. Photograph: Bradley Smith.

Sculptured toys are popular in many countries. They are often made of papier-mâché.

In **papier-mâché**, you create a form by using a watery paste with strips of paper. You build up five or six layers and let the artwork dry. It becomes very stiff and hard.

The sculptures in picture A were made by artists in Japan. The sculptures are used as good luck charms. The tiger is a symbol for good health. The red cow is a charm to keep away the disease of smallpox. Both of these sculptures have heads that move.

You can create a papier-mâché toy or sculpture. Use a cardboard tube for the body. Soak paper in watery paste. Roll the paper to make arms and legs. Add other parts. Cover the whole surface with five or six layers of pasted paper strips.

Unknown, *Servant Doll (Hoko-San),* Japan, 20th century. Painted papier-mâché, 6" (15 cm) tall. Collection of Mingei International. Photograph: Bradley Smith.

C

The two figures in picture B are called Hoko-Sans or servant charms. They are gifts that a bride gives to children. This Hoko-San is a character in a Japanese legend. The legend says:

A poor girl named Omaki became a servant to the daughter of a wealthy samurai, or warrior. The daughter became sick. Omaki drew the disease into her own body and saved the samurai's daughter. Ever since, a Hoko-San or servant charm is placed in bed with a sick child to take away the illness.

  Shaman's Mask, Tlingit Indians, Fort Wrangell, Alaska. Field Museum of Natural History, Chicago, Illinois.

People in many lands create **masks** for special ceremonies. In some lands, people believe a mask will bring spirits that heal people or give them good luck. Some masks are worn to scare away evil spirits.

Masks are a kind of sculpture. The mask in picture A was carved from wood. Then it was painted. The mask was made in Alaska.

Masks and sculpture are **three-dimensional** art. They have height, width and depth.

In many lands, masks are made from wood, clay and other natural materials. Each material may be carefully chosen to add meaning to the mask.

What kinds of masks have you seen or worn? When and why were the masks worn?

You can create a mask from paper. Learn to change the flat paper into a three-dimensional form. Do you see how? Study the ways to shape paper in pictures B and C. What other ways can you make a mask three-dimensional?

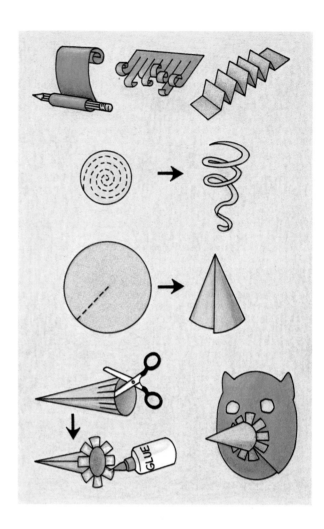

B

1. Think of a shape for the mask. Draw it.

2. Cut out the shape. Add a cut at the bottom.

3. Overlap the paper and paste it down.

4. Your mask will be three-dimensional.

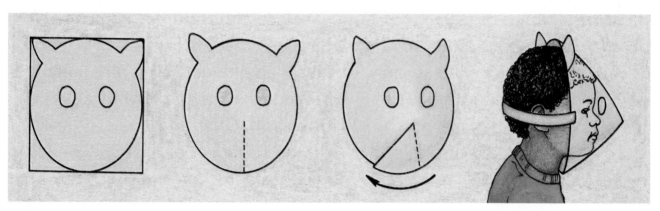

C

50

Jewelry
Modeling Jewelry

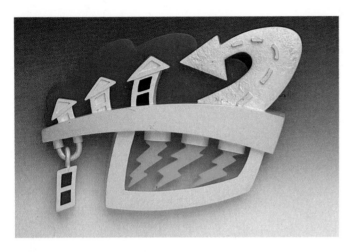

Ruth, Bill and Susan Mahlstedt, *Storm Brooch,* 1989. Sterling silver, acrylic, 2 x 2 3/4" (5 x 7 cm). Courtesy of Moira James Gallery. Photograph: George Post.

Necklace with leaf pendants, ca. 2500 B.C. Gold, lapis lazuli and carneliam. Reproduced by Courtesy of the Trustees of the British Museum, London.

The craft of making jewelry has been done for thousands of years. **Jewelry** includes rings, necklaces, bracelets and earrings. Some kinds of jewelry are useful. Buttons, belt buckles and identification pins are examples. Can you name other kinds of jewelry?

Ideas for jewelry can come from things you see or imagine. Ideas can come from the materials you have and learn to use. The pin, or brooch, in picture A was made by cutting out flat shapes from metal. What theme or idea does the design express?

Ideas for jewelry can come from many sources. The gold necklace in picture B has a repeated pattern of leaf shapes. The idea came from nature. The veins in the leaf are embossed, or pressed down, into the metal.

Since ancient times, some jewelry has been made from rare or beautiful materials like gold. The rare materials helped to make the jewelry a symbol of wealth. Other materials for jewelry can be symbols. For example, on some Pacific Islands, colorful shells and fish teeth are made into jewelry. The jewelry is worn to bring good luck in fishing.

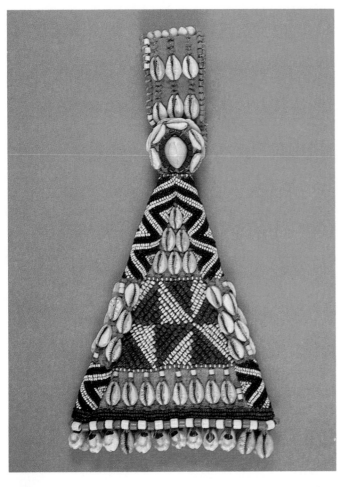

Kuba belt ornament, Zaire, ca. 1890–1910.
Raffia, beads, cowrie shells, 10" (25 cm). Courtesy
of the Peachblown Collection.

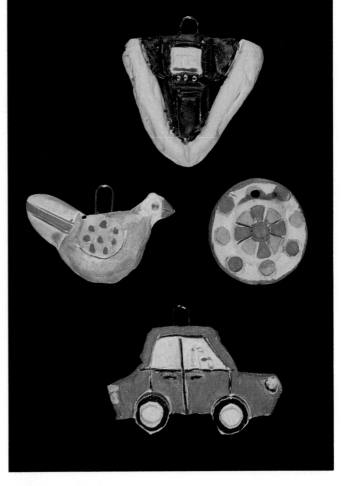

Student artwork.

The belt ornament in picture C is made from shells, beads, and long, thin grass called **raffia**. These ornaments are made by the Kuba people in Zaire, Africa. The ornaments are worn during ceremonial dances. Most of the shells and beads in this ornament are arranged in a symmetrical design.

Students made the pendants in picture D. They used different ideas to begin their designs. Which pendants have ideas that come from nature? What other ideas can you identify?

These pendants are made from a clay-like dough. The neckstring goes through a hole in the clay or a paper clip inserted in the clay. Do you see the embossed parts of each design?

What kind of jewelry can you design? What ideas can you use?

51

Clothing
Designing a Special Hat

B **Unknown,** *Gingasa,* Japan, 19th century. Papier-mâché hat, 10 1/2 " (27 cm) high. Collection of Yamane Washi Shiryokan, Tottori, Japan.

A ***Man's Hat***, Kuba, Zaire, 1890. Cowrie shells, beads, raffia, cloth, brass, 8" (20 cm) diameter. Hampton University Museum. Photograph courtesy of The Center for African Art. Photograph: Jerry L. Thompson.

People around the world create and wear hats. Sometimes hats are worn for practical reasons. For example, a hat can keep you warm or protect you from the sun. The hats you see in this lesson were made in many lands. They are used for special reasons in each culture.

In Zaire, Africa, people who want attention and respect wear hats, such as the one you see in picture A. The hat is decorated with beads, small shells and tiny bells.

The hat in picture B is worn for a festival in Japan. It is made from **papier-mâché**. Have you seen similar hats of paper? When and why are they worn?

An African-American artist made the hat in picture C. The design is inspired by African beadwork.

A Haida artist from the region of British Columbia, Canada made the woven straw hat in picture D. The design on it is a crest. A **crest** is a family symbol.

Xenobia Bailey, *Royal Crown #5*, 1985. Acrylic yarn and mixed media, 7 1/4 x 6 3/4" (18 x 17 cm). Schomburg Center for Research in Black Culture, Art & Artifacts Division. The New York Public Library (Astor, Lenox and Tilden Foundations). Photograph: Frank Stewart.

Cedar Bark Hat, ca. 1890. Painted raven design, Haida, British Columbia, Canada. Courtesy of The National Museum of the American Indian, New York.

Picture E shows some ways to begin a hat design. Create a design that helps people know what the hat means.

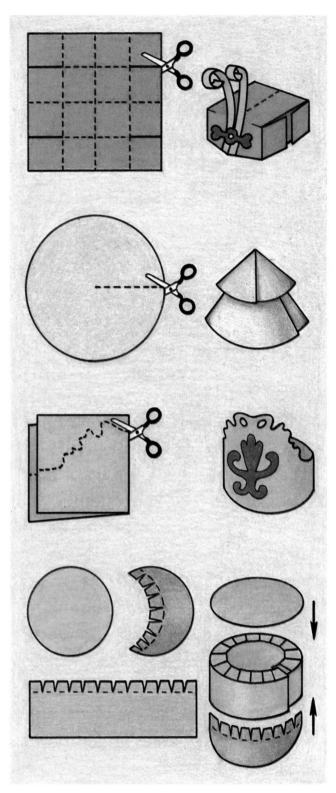

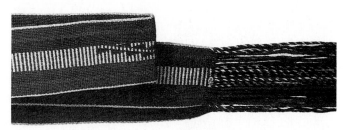

B   **Unknown,** *Navajo-style Sash,* ca. 1965–70, Hopi Indian Reservation, Second Mesa, Arizona. Cotton, 9' 2 3/4" x 4 1/4" (281 x 11 cm). Photograph: Bobby Hansson.

A   **Unknown,** *Kente cloth,* 20th century, Ghana, Ashanti, Africa. Photograph: Jacqueline Robinson.

Thousands of years ago, people learned to weave cloth, or fabrics, for clothes. **Fabrics** are made up of many threads or yarns woven together.

Weaving is done by placing yarns over and under other yarns. Many weavers use a **loom**, or frame, to hold one set of yarns. The yarns on the loom are called the warp. The **warp** threads go up and down on the loom.

The next step in weaving is done with long yarn, called the **weft**. The weft is placed over and under the warp on the loom. Each row of the weft is pressed together so the fabric is tightly woven.

The fabric in picture A is **Kente cloth**. It is made from narrow bands of woven cloth that are stitched together. Kente cloth was first made for African chiefs of the Ashanti Kingdom about 300 years ago.

A Navajo Indian wove the sash in picture B. A sash has very long warp yarns. The colors and patterns in this sash are a traditional design for the Navajo Indians.

You can weave a sash, headband or bracelet. Use a straw loom, such as the one you see on the next page.

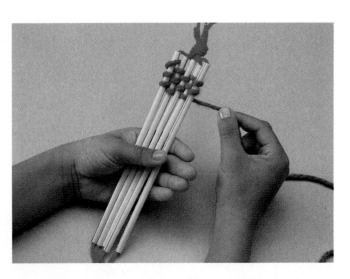

1. Cut five pieces of yarn. Push each yarn through a straw and tie a thick knot at one end.

2. Tie the other ends together in one big knot. Use a long piece of yarn. Weave over and under.

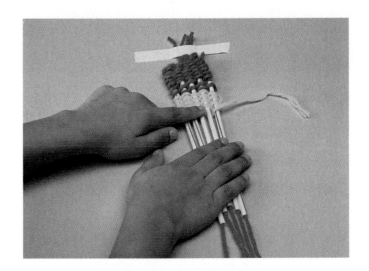

3. Push the weaving up toward the big knot. Pull the straws down.

4. Cut the knots and remove the straws. Tie the loose ends of yarn together.

53

Batik
Designs on Fabric

 Sissi Siska, *Butterflies* (detail). Batik, 20 x 20" (51 x 51 cm). Courtesy of the artist.

Have you ever seen cloth that has a batik design? **Batik** is a process of using wax and dye to make pictures or patterns on cloth. **Dye** is a colored liquid that stains cloth.

Look at the batik in picture A. The white areas show the color of the cloth before it was dyed. All of the white areas were covered with wax. The wax kept the dye from staining the white cloth. Do you know why?

All of the colored areas in the batik were dyed. This batik was waxed and dyed many times to create the rich layers of color.

Batik is a traditional way to decorate cloth in Asia and in parts of Africa. It is also a **technique**, or method, that many artists use today. Batik is called a **resist** process. The dye rolls off, or resists, the wax just like water rolls off a waxed car. Many

 Yardage from a woman's coat, design called Three Wintry Friends, Japan, Edo Period, 1615–1868. Silk, satin and twill weaves, 172 x 162" (437 x 411 cm). ©1991 Indianapolis Museum of Art.

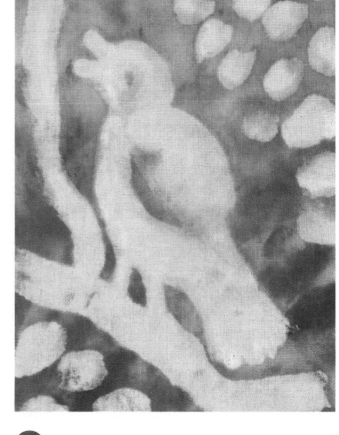

batik designs have a fine pattern of irregular lines. These lines come from the stiff wax. When the cloth is crumpled and put into the dye, the wax cracks. The dye goes into these cracks. This crackle pattern is part of the design.

You can create a batik-like design on white cloth. Your resist medium will be toothpaste mixed with hand lotion. You will use tempera paint instead of dye.

Plan a simple design. Brush the resist medium on the cloth where you want white lines or shapes. Let the cloth dry overnight.

With a sponge brush, gently apply tempera paint over the whole cloth. Wait about five minutes so that the paint has time to stain the cloth. Then rinse the cloth under running water.

54

Modeling Clay
Sculptures of Animals

A

Figurine of Horse and Rider, Greece, 600–550 B.C. Terra-cotta, 4 1/4" (11 cm) high. Museum of Art & Archaeology, University of Missouri, Columbia (Gift of Mr. & Mrs. Stanley Marcus).

B

Figurine of Horse and Rider, Greece, 600–550 B.C. Terra-cotta, 6 1/2" (17 cm) high. Museum of Art & Archaeology, University of Missouri, Columbia (Gift of Mr. & Mrs. Stanley Marcus).

Over 2,000 years ago in Greece, artists created the sculptures in pictures A and B. The horses and riders differ in style. One horse has smooth flowing forms. The other is geometric and decorated with a pattern. Why do you think the artists created sculptures about horses with riders?

The sculptures in pictures A, B and C are made from ceramic clay. In Lesson 46, you learned that **ceramic** clay is a special kind of moist earth and water used to make pottery. It is easy to model into a sculpture. When the sculpture is finished, it is allowed to dry.

The dry sculpture is then fired in a kiln to make the sculpture stronger and more **permanent**. A permanent sculpture will last for a very long time.

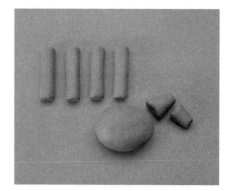

 Horse, China, Tang Dynasty, 7th–8th century. Glazed earthenware, 17 3/4 x 6 x 18 1/4" (45 x 15 x 46 cm). The Brooklyn Museum, New York (Exchange). Photograph: Justin Kerr.

An artist created the sculpture in picture C about 1,200 years ago in China. Sculptures like these were placed in or near graves as memorials to important people. Why do you think the horse is shown without a rider?

This sculpture has been glazed. Glaze adds color to the sculpture and makes it waterproof.

The sculptures in pictures A, B and C have the same subject, but they have different styles. See if you can create a sculpture in your own style. Create an animal. You might add a person to your work. Start with the main forms, then add details and textures.

If you use ceramic clay, join the pieces of clay with slip. **Slip** is a watery mixture of clay with a few drops of vinegar. It helps the pieces of clay stick together.

As you work, turn your sculpture so you can study the forms from all sides. What style will your sculpture have?

Sculptures can be made in different ways. The sculptures in pictures A and D are made from **bronze**, a strong metal. A bronze sculpture is first made in a soft, waxy clay or similar material. The first version is called a **model**.

The sculpture in picture A was made by making a model. The model was planned with many smooth, simple forms. Notice how the artist made thick forms for the arms and legs. The forms fit together tightly. The parts that touch other parts have smooth joints.

Notice how the artist has suggested movement. Where do the arms and legs bend? Can you make a sculpture of people with bends that show action?

 Henry Moore, *Family Group,* 1948–1949. Bronze, 59 1/4 x 46 1/2 x 29 1/4" (151 x 118 x 75 cm). Collection, The Museum of Modern Art, New York (A. Conger Goodyear Fund).

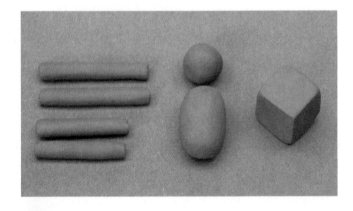

C

Sculpture also can be **modeled**, or shaped, from one large piece of clay. You can pinch and pull the solid clay to create a head and other parts of the sculpture.

The bronze sculpture in picture D has a solid, cone-shaped form. The solid form helps make it strong. Notice the folds in the long gown. The curved folds create a **path of movement** for the eye to follow. Your eyes move around the form even though the figure seems to sit very quietly.

Make a clay sculpture of a person. Will you begin with separate pieces of clay or model a figure from one main form?

 Anne Whitney, *Roma,* 1890. Bronze. Collection of Wellesley College Museum, Wellesley, Massachusetts (Gift of the Class of 1886).

E

 B   **Leone Battista Alberti,** *Self-Portrait,* 1435. Bronze, 7 7/8 x 5 1/2 " (20 x 14 cm). National Gallery of Art, Washington, DC (Samuel H. Kress Collection).

A   **Alfred Lenz,** *Indian,* ca. 1920. Bronze. Post Road Gallery, Larchmont, New York.

The sculptures in this lesson are designed so you see one main view. They are relief sculptures. You see **low relief** sculptures on coins with parts that are raised up from the background. In a **high relief** sculpture, thick forms stand out from the background.

The portraits in pictures A and B are realistic. The **profile**, or side view, on the sculpture in picture A is based on a photograph by Edward Curtis. Edward Curtis was one of the first artists to photograph North American Indians.

The self-portrait in picture B was created by a well-known artist and architect, Alberti. He lived in Italy during the Renaissance (1400-1600).

Jacques Sicard, *Weller Pottery Works, portrait plaque,* late 19th century. Metallic lusterware, 16 3/4 x 13" (43 x 33 cm). National Museum of American History, Smithsonian Institution, Washington, DC.

Picture C is an idealized portrait. In an **idealized portrait**, the artist makes a person's eyes and other features look more perfect or beautiful than they really are. The hairstyle and clothing in this portrait were popular in the United States during the 1800s.

African-American artist Selma Burke created the **realistic** portrait on the United States dime. President Roosevelt sat very still while she created a clay model.

Sketch the profile of a person. Then create a relief sculpture. Roll out a slab of clay. Trim it to make a background shape. Carve and model the clay to make your relief sculpture.

131

57 Carving Clay
Animal Sculpture

Cleo Hartwig, *Quail,* 1973. Marble, 9 1/2 x 11 x 5 1/2" (24 x 28 x 14 cm). Courtesy of Albert Glinsky. Photograph: Walter Russell.

Carving is one of many ways to create sculpture. Carving is called a **subtractive** process because you take away material from a solid block. The block is usually stone or wood. It can be dry clay or plaster. In some cultures, artists carve pieces of bone, gourds and shells.

Cleo Hartwig carved the bird in picture A. She says she tries for "a **stylized**, or simple, interpretation of small animals and birds." The stone that she carved had a form similar to the outline in picture C. Notice the shaded areas in picture C. They show the first parts to be carved away. Why are these parts carved first?

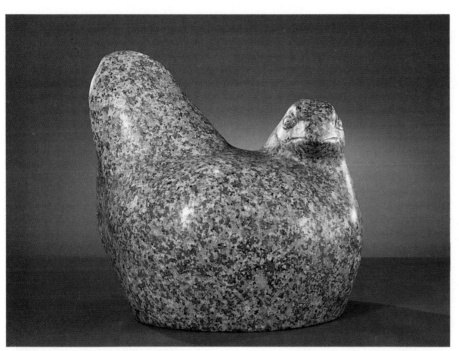

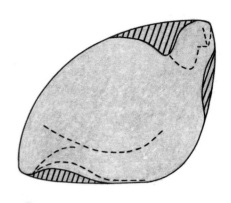

B **William Zorach, *Setting Hen,*** 1946. Granite, 14 1/4 x 15 3/8 x 13 7/8" (36 x 39 x 35 cm). Hirshhorn Museum and Sculpture Garden, Smithsonian Institution, Washington, DC (Gift of Joseph H. Hirshhorn, 1966).

William Zorach's sculpture in picture B also has simple forms. He often carved smooth stones from the rocky coast of New England. Picture D shows some of the carved areas for *Setting Hen*.

Both of these sculptures are abstract. **Abstract** means that the forms are simplified. You do not see many details. The artist gives you the idea of each bird but has not included everything you might see in a real bird.

You can practice carving. Begin with a smooth lump of clay. Imagine it is a smooth rock that you will carve. Study the form to get an idea for a bird or another animal. Create a simple, abstract sculpture. Carve your clay with a paper clip.

133

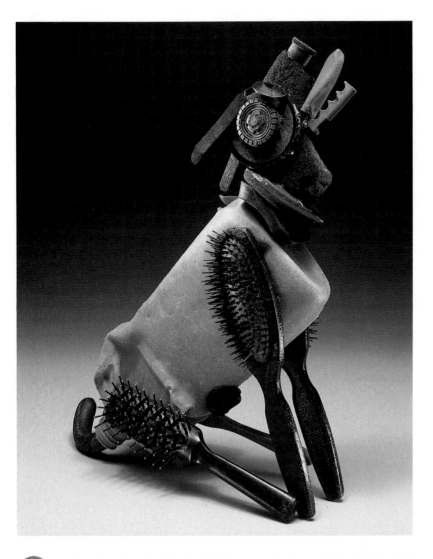

A   **Jerry Ross Barrish,** *Citroên,* 1989. Found plastic objects, 14 1/2 x 11 1/2 x 5 1/2 " (37 x 29 x 14 cm). Courtesy of the artist. Photograph ©1989 Mel Schockner.

B   **Marcel Duchamp,** *Bicycle Wheel,* 1951. Metal and wood, 50 1/2 x 25 1/2 x 6 5/8 " (128 x 43 x 65 cm). Collection, The Museum of Modern Art, New York (The Sidney and Harriet Janis Collection).

Sculptures can be created from scrap materials and objects people discard. In the last eighty years or so, some artists have made sculpture from a variety of objects and materials. They find things to recycle and assemble into works of art. What recycled objects can you identify in picture A?

Marcel Duchamp was one of the first artists to use **ready-made objects** and furniture for sculpture. He wanted people to think about the objects in his sculpture in new ways. He wanted people to think about whether these objects can be art. Do you think this sculpture is art?

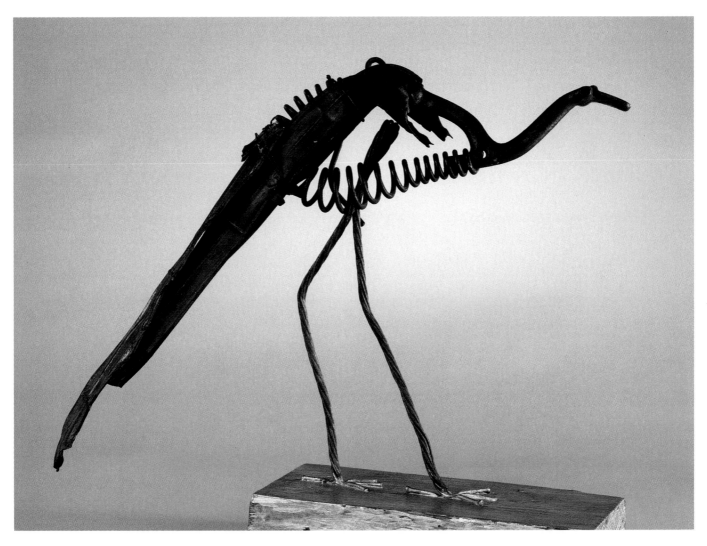

José de Creeft, *Bird,* 1927. Found objects, 11 1/4 x 13 3/8 x 2 1/2" (29 x 34 x 6 cm). Hirshhorn Museum and Sculpture Garden, Smithsonian Institution, Washington, DC (Gift of Joseph H. Hirshhorn, 1966).

José de Creeft was one of the first artists to weld pieces of scrap metal together. He found some of his metal forms in junk yards. His work inspired many other artists to assemble sculptures from metal.

A sculpture created by joining objects is called an assemblage. An **assemblage** is made by finding and collecting objects with interesting forms and textures.

Collect and assemble some objects to create a sculpture. Look for broken toys, clocks and other small objects. Save empty boxes, tubes, bottle caps and buttons. Use your imagination to create an assemblage.

135

 Adrián Luis González, *Typewriter,* 20th century. Painted pottery, 4 3/8" (11 cm) wide. Collection of Chloë Sayer. Photograph: David Lavender.

There are many styles of sculpture. About forty years ago, some artists in England and North America began to create art based on popular culture. Popular culture includes many things people see or buy in stores. In **Pop art**, or popular art, artists get ideas by studying advertising and manufactured objects, such as shoes.

The sculptures in this lesson are examples of the Pop art style. Pop art is now a style in other countries where people see or buy many things in stores. An artist in Mexico created the sculpture in picture A. The typewriter is made of clay. Why might some people enjoy or want to own this artwork? Would you? Why or why not?

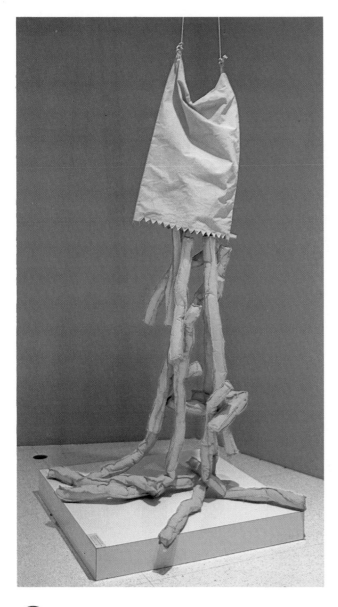

B Claes Oldenburg, *Shoestring Potatoes Spilling from a Bag,* 1966. Canvas, kapok, glue, acrylic, 108 x 46 x 42 " (224 x 117 x 107 cm). Collection Walker Art Center, Minneapolis (Gift of the T.B. Walker Foundation).

The sculpture in picture B is inspired by the forms of food. Have you ever stopped to look at food as sculpture? Why do you think this artist created such a large sculpture? Why do you think he made it from cloth?

C Victor Spinski, *Covered Pail,* 1979. Handbuilt cast whiteware, 13 x 15 " (33 x 38 cm). Courtesy of the artist.

Pop artists usually create sculptures that look like real objects. They study the forms and proportions of the objects they see. The sculptures are also unlike real objects in several ways. How is the sculpture in picture C unlike a real garbage can?

Create a sculpture. Show a manufactured object or food. You might use clay or papier-mâché. After you complete your sculpture, explain how it is similar to the actual object. Explain why it is different.

Your Art Heritage
Latin American Sculptors

Artists from many lands have become well-known in this century. In this lesson you see sculptures by three artists of Latin American **heritage**. The artists speak Spanish or other languages that came from Latin, an ancient language in Europe.

After you learn about these artists, do some research on art from one country, region or heritage. Your teacher and librarians can help you begin. You might do research on artists who share your own heritage.

A

Marisol (Escobar), *The Generals,* 1961–1962. Wood and mixed media, 87 x 28 1/2 x 76" (221 x 72 x 193 cm). Albright-Knox Art Gallery, Buffalo, New York (Gift of Seymour H. Knox, 1962).

The sculpture in picture A was created by Marisol Escobar. She was born in Paris, France, but she grew up in Venezuela, South America. She now lives in New York City.

Many of Marisol's ideas for sculpture come from ancient art in the Americas and from old objects she collects. Many of her artworks are humorous combinations of ideas and materials.

 Luis Jiménez, Jr., *Howl,* 1986. Fiberglas®, 60 x 30 x 30" (152 x 76 x 76 cm). Courtesy Phillis Kind Gallery, New York-Chicago.

C **Joaquín Torres-García,** *Untitled,* 1931. Construction on wood, 19 7/8 x 9 1/8 x 3 7/8" (50 x 23 x 10 cm). Hirshhorn Museum and Sculpture Garden, Washington, DC (Gift of Joseph H. Hirshhorn, 1972).

Luis Jiménez is a Mexican-American artist. *Howl* is one of many sculptures he has created to compare the life of people to the life of animals. This animal has a hard life, but it shows a free spirit whenever it howls.

Joaquín Torres-García was born in Uruguay, South America. He was a painter and a sculptor. He decided to combine these two kinds of art. He loved earth-colors such as browns and grays. He taught many Latin American artists to explore new kinds of art.

 Courtesy of Americans All.

The students in picture A made **quilts** about their friends, families and heritages. They are participating in a special show of quilted art in their hometown.

The artist in picture B is getting ready for an art show. She created the paintings on the wall and the sculpture. She is fixing a light so her artwork will be easy to see.

When artists have a show, they choose their best work. They display it neatly and invite people to see the show. The room or space for an art show is called an **art gallery**.

Your class can have an art show. Everyone should have artwork in the **exhibit**. You should decide which of your own artworks are best. What should you think about while you are deciding?

 B   Courtesy of The School of the Art Institute of Chicago.

Display your artwork on a **mount**, or background paper. The mount should be about 1/2" (1 cm) larger than your artwork. Center the artwork on the mount so the borders are parallel or even, as shown in picture C. On a separate index card, make a label for your artwork. What other plans need to be made? Who will you invite to the show?

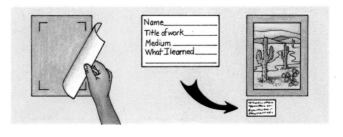

C

Art Safety

Study these safety points. Follow other safety points your teacher tells you about.

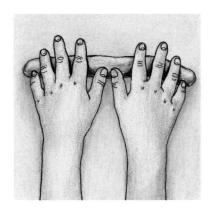

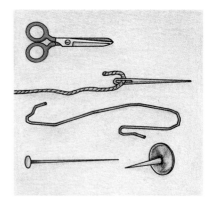

1. If you feel sick or have a health problem, tell your teacher. For example, if you have a rash or scratches on your hands, you should not use clay until your skin heals.

2. Make sure your art materials have a label that says nontoxic. Nontoxic means the materials are safe to use. Read any words that say "Caution." Find out what the words mean.

3. Some tools and materials have sharp points or edges. Use these very carefully. Make sure the sharp objects are pointing away from your body.

4. Use all art tools and materials with care. Keep the tools and materials away from your eyes, mouth and face.

5. Learn to use art materials neatly. After art lessons, wash your hands to remove paint, clay or other materials. Always wash your hands before you eat food.

6. If you drop or spill something, quietly help to clean it up. A wet floor or a floor with pieces of art materials on it can be unsafe to walk on.

Ways to Help in Art

Study these examples of ways to help in the artroom. What else can you do to help?

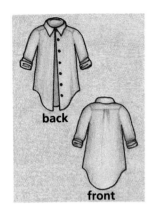

1. Help everyone get ready for art. For some lessons, wear an apron or an old shirt. Button the shirt in the back and roll up the sleeves.

2. Help to clean up. Stack and put art materials away neatly. Wash brushes and store them with the hairs pointing up.

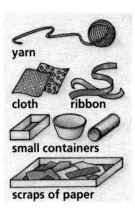

3. Share art tools and materials. Save materials you can use again. You can recycle some materials to create art.

4. Save your artwork in a portfolio. Write your name and the date on all of your sketches and other work. This will help you see and know what you are learning.

5. When you discuss art, listen carefully. Think about what people say. Ask thoughtful questions. In art, there is usually more than one answer to questions.

6. Learn to use art words. Use a dictionary or the glossary on pages 148-154 to find the meaning of art words. Why should you learn art words?

Artists and Artworks

Glossary

Abstract Expressionism (AB-strakt ek-SPRESH-un-ism). A style of art. The artist abstracts, or leaves out, details and tries to capture the main action or feeling in a subject.

abstract (AB-strakt). A style of art in which the artist often adds or omits elements in an observed scene to create a simple design.

analogous (ah-NAL-uh-gus). A color scheme planned around colors that are next to each other on the color wheel, such as yellow-green, yellow and yellow-orange.

analyze (AN-uh-lize). In art, seeing and thinking about principles of design that are used to plan an artwork.

angle (ANG-gul). A bend in a line or shape.

animator (an-ah-MAY-tur). An artist who draws the pictures for cartoon-like motion pictures.

appliqué (ah-plee-KAY). Artwork that is made by sewing pieces of cloth onto a cloth background.

architect (AR-ki-tekt). An artist who designs buildings.

armature (AR-muh-chur). A wire or stiff support that is placed inside a sculpture to hold it up.

art. A form of visual communication and expression.

art gallery (art GAL-uh-ree). A building, or a space in a building, where artworks are shown.

assemblage (ah-SEM-blij). Sculpture made by joining objects, or parts of objects, together.

asymmetrical (AY-sih-met-rick-ul). Having visual balance when the parts are arranged differently on each side of an artwork.

asymmetry (ay-SIM-e-tree). A type of visual balance in which the parts are arranged differently on each side.

background (BAK-ground). In a scene or an artwork, the part that looks farther away or behind other parts.

balcony (BAL-kuh-nee). A porch-like platform anywhere above the first floor of a building.

batik (bah-TEEK). A process of using wax and dye to make pictures or patterns on cloth.

block (blok). A thick form or material with flat surfaces.

bronze (bronz). A metal that is a mixture of copper and tin.

career (kah-REER). A job in art that requires special skills and education.

caricature (KAR-ah-kuh-chur). An artwork that exaggerates how something actually looks, usually humorous.

cartoon (kar-TOON). A drawing meant to be humorous.

center of interest (SEN-ter of IN-trist). The main, or first, thing you notice in an artwork.

ceramic clay (sir-AM-ik klay). A form of earth mixed with water that can be shaped and fired to create permanent artwork.

cityscape (SIT-ee-skape). Artwork that shows a city.

close-up (KLOSE-up). Artwork in which objects look very near.

collage (koh-LAHZH). Artwork made by pasting pieces of paper or other materials to a flat surface.

color scheme (KOL-er skeem). A plan for using colors. (*see* analogous, complementary)

complementary colors (kom-pleh-MEN-tuh-ree KOL-ers). Colors that are opposite from each other on the color wheel. Pairs of colors, such as red and green, yellow and violet, or orange and blue.

composition (*see* design)

contour (KON-toor). The edge of a shape.

contrast (KON-trast). A great difference between two things.

cool colors (kool KOL-ers). Colors that remind people of cool things. Varieties of blue, green and violet.

courtyard (kort-yard). A roofless, garden-like space inside a building.

craft. Skill in creating things by hand. Artwork created carefully by hand.

craftsworker (KRAFTS-wor-ker). A highly skilled person who creates artwork by hand.

crayon etching (KRAY-on ECH-ing). A process of scratching through one layer of crayon to let another layer of crayon show.

crest. A set of visual symbols for a family, tribe or other group of people.

design (de-ZINE). A plan for arranging the parts or elements of an artwork. An artwork which has a planned arrangement of visual elements.

detail (de-TALE or DEE-tale). A small part.

diagonal (die-AG-uh-nal). A line or edge that slants or tilts.

dilute (di-LOOT). Adding a liquid to another liquid to make it thinner or flow more easily.

docent (DO-sent). A guide and teacher for people who visit a museum.

dye. A colored liquid that stains the threads in a fabric.

editorial cartoon (ed-i-TORE-ee-ul car-TOON). A drawing or other artwork in which an artist expresses an opinion about society.

elements of design (EL-uh-ments of de-ZINE). Parts of an artwork that an artist plans. These elements are line, color, texture, value, space and shape.

embroidery (em-BROY-duh-ree). A decoration on fabric made with a needle and thread.

emphasis (EM-fuh-sis). A principle of design in which some visual elements are given more importance than others to attract and keep a viewer's attention.

exhibit (eg-ZIB-it). A display of artwork.

Expressionism (ek-SPRESH-un-ism). A style of artwork in which the main idea is to show a definite mood or feeling.

expressionist (ek-SPRESH-un-ist). Artworks that portray a strong feeling or definite mood.

fabric (FAB-rik). Cloth made of many threads or yarns woven or layered together.

fantasy art (FAN-tah-see art). Artwork that is meant to look unreal, strange or dream-like.

fiber art (FIE-bur art). Artwork created from long, thin, thread-like materials.

firing (FIE-er-ing). The process of hardening a clay object by exposing it to great heat.

foreground (FOR-ground). In a scene or picture, the part that seems near or close to you.

form. An element of design. Forms are three-dimensional, such as a cube, sphere or cylinder. They have height, width and thickness. Forms are not flat.

formal design (FOR-mal de-ZINE). Artwork that has parts arranged the same way on both sides. Also called symmetrical design.

geometric (gee-oh-MEH-trik). A shape or form that has smooth, even edges.

glaze (glayz). A mixture of water and colored minerals applied to ceramics. When a glazed work is fired, the minerals melt and create a glassy coating.

graphic designer (GRAF-ik de-ZINE-er). An artist who plans the lettering and artwork for books, posters and other printed materials.

guideline (GIDE-line). A line, folded edge or other mark that serves as a guide for planning an artwork.

heritage (HER-i-tij). The history and culture of a group of people.

high relief (hie re-LEEF). In sculpture, the raised forms that stand out highest from a background.

horizontal (hor-i-ZON-tal). A straight line that lies flat.

hue (hyoo). The common name for a color, such as red, yellow, blue, orange, green, violet.

human-made environment (HYOO-man-made en-VIE-run-ment). Parts of the environment and objects that are shaped by humans or changed from their natural state.

idealized portrait (i-DEE-uh-lized POR-tret). A likeness of a person whose features have been changed to look more perfect than they really are.

illusion (ih-loo-zhun). In art, a design that causes you to think an image is the real thing.

illustrator (IL-uh-stray-ter). An artist who creates pictures for books and magazines, etc.

imagination (ih-maj-uh-NAY-shun). The process of creating a mental picture of something that is unlike things one has seen.

Impressionism (im-PRESH-un-ism). A style of art in which the main idea is to show changes in the light, color or activity of scenes.

industrial designer (in-DUS-tree-al de-ZINE-er). An artist who designs cars, dishes, toys and other products that are made in factories.

informal design (in-FOR-mal de-ZINE). Artwork that looks balanced when parts are arranged differently on each side. Also called asymmetrical design.

interior designer (in-TEER-ee-ur de-ZINE-er). An artist who plans the inner spaces of a building.

intermediate colors (in-ter-MEE-dee-it KOL-erz). Colors that are made from a primary and a secondary color, such as red-orange and yellow-orange.

invented texture (in-VENT-ed TEKS-chur). A texture made by an artist that reminds you of a texture you could actually touch.

inventive (in-VEN-tiv). Able to think of ideas that no one else has thought about.

jewelry (JOO-el-ree). Objects such as rings, necklaces, bracelets and earrings that are worn for personal adornment.

Kente cloth (KIN-tay klawth). Woven strips of ceremonial cloth used for scarfs and robes in the Ivory Coast, Africa.

kiln (kill). A special oven or furnace that can be heated to a high temperature.

landmark (LAND-mark). Something (a building, a statue, a park) that is easy to see and important to people in a community.

landscape (LAND-skape). Artwork that shows an outdoor scene.

landscape architect (LAND-skape AR-ki-tekt). An artists who plans parks, gardens and other outdoor spaces.

lettering (LET-er-ing). Drawing the shapes of the letters of the alphabet.

loom. A frame used to hold yarns while weaving.

low relief (low ree-LEEF). A sculptural form in which parts of the design stand up slightly from from the background.

mask. An artwork used to cover and disguise a face.

masterpiece (MAS-ter-pees). An artwork that many people have admired for a long time.

materials (ma-TEER-ee-alz). The basic things one needs to make an artwork, such as wood or paint.

middle ground (MID-al ground). The space that appears to lie between the foreground and background of a painting.

model (MOD-el). A person who poses for an artist. Also, a small artwork that shows how a larger artwork might look.

modeled (MOD-eld). Shaped or formed, such as a piece of clay that is made into a sculpture.

monoprint (MON-oh-print). A print that is usually limited to one copy.

mosaic (moh-ZAY-ik). Artwork made with small pieces of colored stone, glass or the like.

mosque (mosk). A building of worship for people who practice the religion of Islam (or Muslim faith).

motion (MOH-shun). Movement, either real or visual.

mount. Paper or cardboard on which a picture is pasted to make a border around it.

movement (MOOV-ment). Going from one place to another or a feeling of action in an artwork.

natural environment (NACH-ur-al en-VIH-run-ment). A setting in nature that has not been changed by humans.

natural shape (NACH-ur-al shape). A shape, usually without perfectly straight lines, that occurs in nature. Also called an organic shape.

negative shape or space (NEG-eh-tiv shape or space). A shape or space surrounding a line, shape or form. (*See* background)

neutral colors (NEW-trel KOL-ers). In artwork, neutral colors are brown, black, white and gray.

organic (or-GAN-ik). Organic forms are similar to forms in nature and usually have curved or irregular edges.

outdoor sculpture (out-door SKULP-chur). Sculpture intended for display in the outdoors.

overlap (o-ver-LAP). One shape behind another.

palette (PAL-it). A tray-like surface for mixing colors.

papier-mâché (PAY-per ma-SHAY). The process of building up a form with strips of paper dipped in a watery paste. When the layers of pasted paper dry, the artwork is firm and hard.

path of movement (path of MOOV-ment). Lines that guide the eye over and through different areas of an artwork.

pattern (PAT-urn). A choice of lines, colors or shapes, repeated over and over in a planned way. Also, a model or guide for making something.

permanent (PER-mah-nent). Something that lasts for a very long time.

perspective (per-SPEK-tiv). Artwork in which the spaces and distances between objects look familiar or "real."

photograph (FOH-toh-graf). A picture made by using a camera.

photogram (FOH-toh-gram). A record of shadows that is made on a special photographic paper. The paper changes when light strikes it.

photographer (foh-TOG-ruh-fur). A person who takes photographs using a camera.

Pop art. A style of artwork that includes advertisements or other popular, familiar images.

pose (pohz). A special way to stand or sit.

positive shape or space (POZ-i-tiv shape or space). A shape or space that you see first because it contrasts, or stands out from, the background.

pottery (POT-er-ee). A container created by hand from ceramic clay.

pre-Columbian (pree-koh-LUM-bee-an). Art created before Christopher Columbus and other Europeans came to the Americas.

primary colors (PRI-mer-ee KOL-ers). The three colors of red, yellow and blue from which all other colors can be made. (In light, the primary colors are red, green and blue.)

principles of design (PRIN-sih-pals of de-ZINE). Guides for planning relationships among visual elements in artworks. Principles of design are balance, rhythm, proportion, pattern, unity and variety.

print. To produce copies of images, usually by pressing ink onto paper.

product designer (PROD-ukt de-ZINE-er). An artist who plans the appearance of factory-made products, such as cars, furniture, kitchen ware.

profile (PROH-file). Something seen or shown in artwork from the side view, such as a profile of a head.

proportion (pro-POR-shun). The size, location or amount of something as compared to that of something else.

quilt (kwilt). A hand-made blanket that is made by sewing pieces of cloth together.

radial (RAY-dee-al). Lines or shapes that spread out from a center point.

radial balance (RAY-dee-al BAL-ens). A design in which the elements are visually connected to a central point.

raffia (RAF-ee-uh). Long, thin grass used for weaving, basketry and other fiber arts.

ready-made objects (RED-ee made OB-jekts). Objects for sculpture assembled from scrap materials or objects that people have discarded.

realism (REE-ah-liz-em). A style of art that shows objects or scenes as they might look in everyday life.

realistic (REE-ah-lis-tic). Art that portrays a familiar subject with lifelike colors, textures, shadows and proportions.

realistic portrait (REE-ah-lis-tic POR-trait). An artwork that shows the likeness of a real person.

related colors (ree-LATE-ed KOL-ers). Colors that are next to each other on a color wheel, such as yellow, yellow-green and yellow-orange. Also called analogous colors.

resist (ri-ZIST). An art process in which two materials do not mix or blend together, such as wax crayons used with watery paint.

scroll (skrohl). A long roll of paper or cloth illustrated with pictures or lettering. Scrolls were used before the invention of books.

seascape (SEE-scape). Artwork that shows a scene of the sea or ocean.

secondary colors (sek-on-dare-ee KOL-ers). Colors which can be mixed from two primary colors; orange, green, violet.

shade. A color mixed by adding black. A dark value of a hue (such as dark or very dark blue).

shading (SHADE-ing). Slight changes in the lightness or darkness of a color or value.

site. The location of something.

sketch (skech). A drawing that is made to record what you see, explore an idea or plan another artwork.

slip. A creamy mixture of clay with water and a few drops of vinegar. It helps pieces of clay stick together.

space. An empty place or surface, or a three-dimensional area that holds something.

stained glass (staynd glass). Pieces of colored glass that are fitted together like parts of a puzzle.

stencil (STEN-sell). A paper or other flat material with a cut-out design that is used for printing. Ink or paint is pressed through the cut-out design onto the surface to be printed.

still life. An artwork that shows non-living things, such as books, candles and so on.

stitchery (STICH-er-ree). Artwork which is made by using a needle and thread or yarn to create stiches on cloth. A stitch is one in-and-out movement of a threaded needle.

structure (STRUK-chur). The supporting parts of an object.

studio (STOO-dee-oh). The place where an artist creates artwork.

style (stile). An artist's special way of creating art.

stylized (STILE-ized). A design based on something you can recognize, but with simple lines and other visual elements.

subject (SUB-jekt). A topic or idea represented in an artwork, such as a landscape or animals.

subtractive (sub-TRAK-tiv). Cutting or taking away the surface to create a form, as in carving wood.

symbol (SIM-bul). Lines, shapes or colors that have a special meaning.

symmetry (SIM-eh-tree). Parts arranged the same way on both sides.

tactile texture (TAK-til TEKS-chur). A texture that you can feel by touch.

technique (tek-NEEK). A special way to create artwork, often by following a special procedure.

texture (TEKS-chur). The way an object feels when it is touched. Also, the way an object looks like it feels, such as rough or smooth.

theme. A story or big idea, such as friendship or faith, that artists can interpet in many ways with different subjects.

three-dimensional (THREE-di-men-chen-al). Artwork that can be measured three ways: height, width, depth (or thickness). Artwork that is not flat.

tint. A light value of a color, such as pink. A color mixed with white.

tower (TOW-er). A tall and slender building or structure.

tradition (tra-DISH-en). The handing down of information, beliefs or activities from one generation to another.

traditional art (*see* tradition).

translucent (trans-LOO-cent). A surface that allows light to pass through, but that does not allow you to see through it clearly.

transparent (trans-PAR-ent). Possible to see through, such as a clear piece of glass.

two-dimensional (TOO-di-MEN-chen-al). Artwork that is flat and is measured in only two ways: height and width.

unique (yu-NEEK). Unlike any others.

unity (YU-ni-tee). Having all the parts of an artwork look as if they belong together or work together like a team.

value (VAL-yu). The lightness or darkness of a color (pink is a light value of red).

vertical (VUR-ti-kul). Lines that go straight up and down.

view (vyew). The position of something when you look at it.

visual rhythm (VIS-yu-al RITH-um). Repeated shapes, colors and other visual elements that remind you of rhythms in music or dance.

visual symbol (VIS-yu-al SIM-bul). Lines, colors and shapes that stand for something else, as a red heart may stand for love.

visual texture (VIS-yu-al TEKS-chur). A surface quality (such as roughness or smoothness) that can be sensed with the eye but not felt.

warm colors (warm KOL-ers). Colors that remind people of warm things. Varieties of red, yellow and orange.

warp. In weaving, the threads or yarns placed on a loom and stretched tightly so that other threads can be woven across them.

watercolor paint (WA-ter-KOL-er paint). Special paints that are mixed with water and look like a watery, transparent ink or stain.

waterproof (WA-ter proof). Water cannot soak into something that is waterproof.

weaving (WEEV-ing). Artwork created by locking together separate strands of material (such as yarn or thread).

weft. Yarn that is woven horizontally over and under the warp on a loom.

Index